SHIPWRECKS

AROUND

WALES

Volume Two

Note: Although reasonable care has been taken in preparing this book, the publisher and author respectively accept no responsibility or liability for any errors, ommissions or alterations, or for any consequences ensuing upon the use of, or reliance upon, any information contained herein described or indicated. The author would be glad to hear of any inaccuracies or any new relevant material.

SHIPWRECKS AROUND WALES

Volume Two

Tom Bennett

 Happy Fish

Published by Happy Fish, Newport, Dyfed, Wales SA42 0UF.

By the same author;

Welsh Shipwrecks, Vol. One, Aberdyfi to St. David's Head. (1981).
Welsh Shipwrecks, Vol. Two, St. David's Head, Pembrokeshire Islands to St. Ann's Head. (1982).
Welsh Shipwrecks, Vol. Three, Milford Haven, St Govan's Head, Tenby and Carmarthen Bay. (1983).
Fishguard Lifeboats. (In aid of RNLI funds, 1984).
Shipwrecks Around Wales. Volume One. (1987).

Printed and bound in Wales.
Typesetting & page layout by Design 29, Dinas Cross, Dyfed.
Printed by Gomer Press, Llandysul, Dyfed.

British Library Cataloguing in Publication Data.
A catalogue record for this book is available
from the British Library.

Bennett, Tom, *1947* -
 Shipwrecks around Wales.
 Vol. 2
 1. Shipwrecks - Wales - History
 I. Title

ISBN 0 9512114 2 0

Contents

The Lifeboat on its carriage

Photographs & Illustrations

Author,
Mr Bryan Andrews of Kelpies,
City of Bristol Museum,
Mr Tony Comley,
Mr Brian Entwistle,
Henry Parry Collection, Gwynedd Archives Service,
Mrs A. Hughes,
Illustrated London News,
Richard Larn Collection,
Manchester Diving Group,
Maritime Museum of the Atlantic, Nova Scotia,
MOD (Navy),
New Quay Town Council,
Norsk Sjofartsmuseum, Oslo,
David Owen,
Trevor Owens Collection,
Pembrokeshire County Museum,
RNLI,
Mr Jim Silk,
Mr Roger Worsley,
Welsh Industrial and Maritime Museum, Cardiff,

The author wishes to thank everyone for their cooperation in providing photographs. Because of the transient nature of shipwrecks and the fact that they often occur at night or in atrocious weather conditions, photographic records of the event are rare. The author is keen to trace as many photographs or postcards of Welsh shipwrecks as possible or alternatively suggest that they should be shown to the nearest County Records Office in order that these historic pictures are not lost to future generations.

Author's Acknowledgements

I would like to thank all who have helped with this book; my wife Maureen, for her diligence in correcting the text, readers and bookshops who have been waiting patiently for this second volume, and a special thanks to diving friends who not only put up with me, but have also provided useful information about the wreck sites; especially Greg Evans and Jim Phillips.

To all those who have kindly let me copy photographs; David Owen of Goodwick, Mrs A. Hughes of Dinas Cross, Bryan Andrews of 'Kelpies', Donald Davies of Cardigan, Ken Williams of Fishguard and Goodwick Historical Society, Brian Entwistle of Rhosneigr, Trevor Owens of Hakin, Gwynedd Archives Service, Pembrokeshire County Museums, Welsh Industrial and Maritime Museum, Cardiff, Maritime Museum of the Atlantic, Nova Scotia, Norsk Sjorfartsmuseum, Oslo, Manchester Diving Group, New Quay Town Council, RNLI, Jim Silk of Malvern, Tony Comley of Porthcawl, George Middleton of St David's, Jim Phillips of Swansea and Greg Evans of Pontardawe. My appreciation is also extended to the staff at The Welsh Industrial and Maritime Museum, Cardiff, Pembrokeshire Records Office and Haverfordwest Library, Diving Services Anglesey and the librarians at the National Library of Wales, Aberystwyth, and Liverpool City Library.

Every endeavour has been made to eliminate errors. If mistakes are found, I apologize and would hope that readers will inform me so that they can be rectified for future editions.

Introduction

For thousands of years seafarers have sailed along the shores of Wales. To reach the port of Liverpool, mariners have had to round the North Wales coast and the treacherous Skerries rocks, and to reach Bristol have had to contend with the Bristol Channel with its gales, shifting sandbanks and strong currents. Throughout the nineteenth century the South Wales ports were some of the busiest in the world, exporting vast quantities of coal. Ships and the sea have been an integral part of the Welsh coastal communities.

The coastal towns not only built strong and seaworthy sailing vessels but also produced some of the most renowned and beloved sea captains.

This book is a collection of over fifty true stories of tragedies at sea, of successful rescues, of men who have lost their lives attempting to save others, and of vessels of all shapes, sizes and nationalities which have been lost around the coast of Wales.

Tom Bennett
January 1992
Newport,
Pembrokeshire.

A finely carved figurehead found floating in Solva harbour around 1840
Photo: Courtesy of Paul Raggett

Location Map of Wrecks in this Book

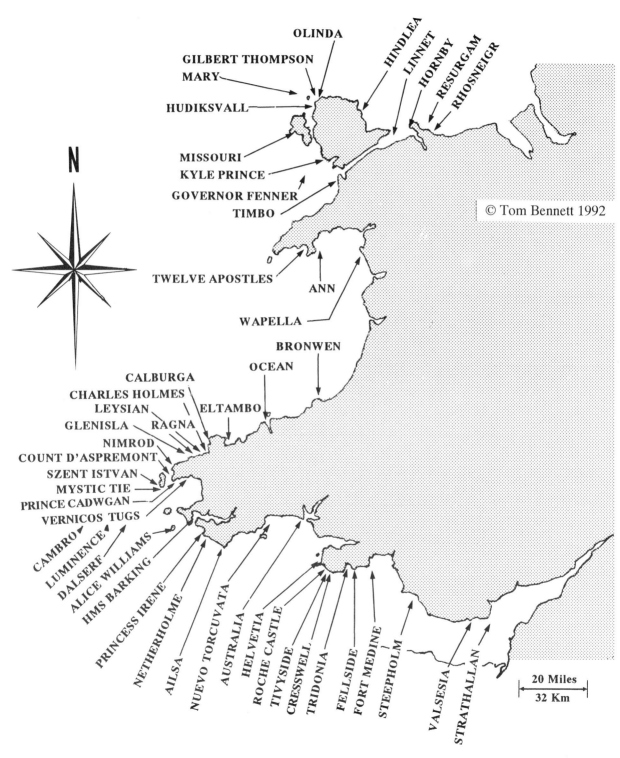

© Tom Bennett 1992

20 Miles
32 Km

AILSA

Type: Cargo Steamship
Port of Registry: Glasgow
Tonnage: 600 tons
Built: 1869, Glasgow
Date of Sinking: 16th November 1880
Location: St Govan's Head, Pembrokeshire, Dyfed

The steamer AILSA was wrecked on the rocks beneath St Govan's Head, on the South Pembrokeshire coast in 1880. The location is most inhospitable, it is remote and beneath towering cliffs and it will come as no surprise to those who know the spot to learn that everyone on board was lost.

The AILSA had left Bristol for Glasgow with a general cargo consisting of iron hoops, lead piping, tanned hides and some 7 passengers. Six of the passengers were actually members of the crew of the ATLAS which had recently arrived from Quebec, and the seventh was a discharged soldier on his way home to Scotland.

The details leading up to the loss of the AILSA will never be known, as there were no surivors to tell the tale and no witnesses of the steamer in trouble. What is known is that there was an almighty November gale during that night and it is supposed that the engine power of the AILSA was insufficient to keep her away from the land.

The steamer was smashed to pieces at the base of the large cliffs and all on board were lost, one assumes by drowning, by being pounded by waves on to the rocks or by the cold water. Over the next few days bodies washed ashore and no less than ten bodies were eventually laid to rest at Bosherston Churchyard.

It took almost two days to ascertain which steamer had been lost. The difficulties being the absence of survivors and the position of the wreckage. The ship was pounded to pieces beneath large cliffs and the only means of getting close to the wreck was by descending on ropes.

THE WRECK OFF ST. GOVAN'S HEAD.

Nov 20 1880

LIST OF THE CREW.

St Govans Head

The Ailsa, wrecked off Milford on Tuesday, left Bristol for Glasgow on Monday afternoon, with a crew of twenty all told, seven passengers, and a general cargo, consisting of iron, hides, &c. The passengers comprised six of the crew of the Atlas, which recently arrived in Bristol from Quebec, and the seventh was a discharged soldier on his way North. The Ailsa was an iron built screw steamer of 600 gross tonnage, built in Glasgow in 1869, and owned by Messrs. Sloan and Co. of Glasgow. It is believed she was overtaken by Tuesday's gale, and driven on the rocks during the night. The captain and crew were : Captain Huckman, of Bristol ; Neil Maclean, chief officer, Glasgow ; Samuel Silcox, quartermaster, Bristol ; James Yates, Bristol ; Thomas Williams, able seaman, Bristol; John Wildon, able seaman, Bristol ; Isaac Hobbs, fireman, Bristol ; Paul Townley, ordinary seaman, Glasgow ; Robert M'Master, chief engineer, Glasgow ; James Hutchinson, second engineer, Glasgow ; Alexander Dodds, winchman, Glasgow ; John Fraser, fireman, Glasgow ; Wm. M'Cann, fireman, Glasgow ; John Leggatt, steward, Glasgow ; John Horner, of Stransaer ; and Henry Peat, ordinary seaman, Bristol. The names of the other four members of the crew are not known in Bristol.

The local newspaper lists the lost crew

A book was found on one of the bodies with the name PRINCESS ALEXANDRA on it, a steamer that plied between Glasgow and Bristol. However that vessel arrived safely in Bristol. A part of the bow wreckage revealed the name AILSA in yellow letters. The AILSA crew similarly did the same Bristol to Glasgow run and almost all the crew were from one or other of those ports.

ALICE WILLIAMS

Type: Sailing Vessel, 2 Masted Schooner
Port of Registry: Falmouth
Official Number: 22780
Tonnage: 132 tons
Built: 1854, Llanelli
Length: 83 feet
Breadth: 23 feet
Date of Sinking: February 24th 1928
Location: Skokholm Island, Pembrokeshire, Dyfed

The ALICE WILLIAMS was a well known topsail schooner that started her life trading to German and Russian ports. Built by Bevans of Llanelli in 1854 this two masted schooner traded for nearly three quarters of a century, an era that saw the replacement of sailing vessels by steam driven ones. She was one of the last trading schooners to be seen with a figurehead and during her considerable lifetime she was greatly admired for her decorated ports and her panelled cabin painted with ships and roses. She was based in Falmouth and many of her trading years were spent in the Welsh slate trade. On her last voyage, however, she was carrying a coal cargo sailing south near Skomer Island in a fog, when she struck a rock.

The ALICE WILLIAMS started to sink by the bow as she neared St Ann's Head. The crew attempted to pump her out but found, to their

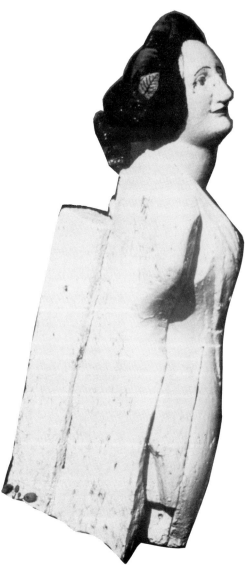

Figurehead of the 'Alice Williams'

dismay, that the pumps were clogged with coal dust. When off St Ann's Head, the large seas caused her to roll heavily. As she was sinking the Captain decided to abandon her.

The 8 crew took to the ship's boat and rowed for the safety of Pembroke. They assumed, when they were leaving her, that their beloved schooner would sink within a few minutes but in the fog the ALICE WILLIAMS had a will of her own. In the southerly breeze, with all sails set, she sailed unmanned towards Skokholm Island where she ran onto the rocks. It was high water on a large tide and as she hit the rocks her bowsprit and figurehead were broken off with the impact and a headsail tore. Ronald Lockley, the farmer and naturalist who lived on the island, was quick to take full advantage of the opportunity to salvage the coal and the schooner's materials. In the fortnight before the schooner broke apart, fifty tons of coal were taken from her hold, and all the spars, sails and rigging were also saved. Good use was made of all the salvaged parts and there was more than enough timber to completely re-roof the farmhouse. A detailed account of the salvage can be read in R.M.Lockley's books *The Way to an Island* and *Dream Island Days*.

A detailed photograph showing the bowsprit, figurehead and forerigging of the ALICE WILLIAMS
Photo: Gwynedd Archives Service

ANN

Type: Sailing Flat, Smack Rigged
Port of Registry: Caernarfon
Tonnage: 60 tons
Built: 1799, Frodsham
Length: 62 feet
Breadth: 15 feet
Date of Sinking: October 18th 1858
Location: St Tudwal's Islands, Gwynedd

The name ANN was a common one for sailing vessels, however this story is about a vessel that is well known amongst lovers of Welsh folk songs but they are unlikely to recognise the name. If the name FFLAT HUW PUW was given instead, it would immediately spring to mind as it is the subject matter for Professor J.Glyn Davies's sea shanties.

Inspired by listening to sea shanties sung by Captain Robert Thomas's all Welsh crew aboard the large square rigged ship MEIRIONETH as she approached the quayside at Liverpool, Glyn Davies collected as many of the shanties as he was able, adding his own words to those where only the tunes remained.

A flat was a flat bottomed sailing barge, once a commonplace cargo carrier on the Mersey. The ANN was a 60 ton flat and her Master was Captain Huw Pugh born in 1795. FFLAT HUW PUW as the vessel is now known through the songs, was wrecked after hitting one of the rocks near St Tudwal's Islands in October 1858. The flat was 59 years old, a considerable age for a working vessel, and she was taking a cargo of timber to Barmouth on her last voyage.

The following is an extract from one of the songs;

Fflat Huw Puw yn hwylio,
Dafydd Jones yn rhiffio;
Huw Puw wrth y llyw,
Yn gweiddi Duw a'n helpo.

Huw Pugh's flat is sailing, Davey Jones is reefing, Huw Pugh is at the tiller, crying out to God to help us.

Author's drawing of a sailing flat

Mae swn ym Mhorthdinllaen swn hwylie'n codi, Blocie gyd yn gwichian Dafydd Jones yn gweiddi. Ni fedra'i aros gartre' yn fy myw; Rhaid i mi fynd yn llongwr iawn ar Fflat Huw Puw.

Music courtesy of Elin Williams

AUSTRALIA

Type: Sailing Ship, 3 Masted Full Rigged
Port of Registry: Christiana, Norway
Previous Name: WILLIAM DOUGLAS
Signal Letters: HFMV
Tonnage: 1,287 tons register
Built: 1875, Maitland, Nova Scotia
Length: 201 feet
Breadth: 40 feet
Date of Sinking: March 30th 1901
Location: Carmarthen Bay, Dyfed

The three masted sailing ship AUSTRALIA was outward bound for Rio de Janeiro when a full westerly gale caused her to turn and run for shelter. The Atlantic gales crippled her and she was flying distress signals when she returned. She was sighted off Caldy Island by the Tenby Coastguards who alerted the Lifeboat crew. The Tenby Lifeboat was launched but the disabled ship was seen heading in the direction of the notorious sandbanks of Cefn Sidan; the Tenby Lifeboat crew returned home and the Ferryside Lifeboat was alerted.

The AUSTRALIA, originally named the WILLIAM DOUGLAS, had a full cargo of coal from Cardiff. The 1,900 tons of coal in her hold caused her to pound heavily against the sandbank when she grounded on the easternmost end of Pendine Sands. The Ferryside Lifeboat was launched at 8.35am and battled under oars and sail to get to the wreck while heavy seas were building up in the shallow water. Despite the size of the AUSTRALIA'S hull the huge seas swept over the decks and through the hatches filling her hold as she settled further into the water, her decks totally awash. Her crew were struggling to stay alive.

Two men failed to hang on to the rigging in the biting cold and were washed into the sea and drowned. The survivors secured themselves in the rigging and awaited rescue. After some skilful manouvering the Lifeboat Coxswain, Dai Jones, managed to get the Lifeboat alongside and 15 men were taken from the washed decks and rigging. During the rescue the Assistant Coxswain of the Lifeboat had a narrow escape when he was washed out of the Lifeboat but was quickly hauled back by his comrades. Dai Jones was awarded a silver medal by the King of Sweden and Norway for this rescue.

Lloyds Weekly Shipping Index conveniently condenses the story, 'She struck at 5.30am, all crew taking to the rigging. Ferryside Lifeboat left at 8.30am, returning to Ferryside at 2pm with 15 of the crew, 2 being drowned. Crew seriously injured, Captain got his arm broken. Ship breaking up quickly, and without doubt will become a total wreck'. Telegram at 5pm states, 'AUSTRALIA now a total wreck, No.2 bank, 10 miles from Ferryside'. So destructive is the power of the waves in Carmarthen Bay that these reports were followed by a telegram five days later which simply said, 'The ship AUSTRALIA has entirely disappeared'.

The coal from the wreck gradually spread over the whole area and washed ashore for many years providing winter fuel for those who took the time to collect it.

The Norwegian barque AUSTRALIA lying quietly at anchor. Note the sailor aloft on the foremast and also the circular plates on the mooring ropes aft to prevent rats climbing along them.
The AUSTRALIA was wrecked on the eastermost end of Pendine Sands in March 1901.

Photo: Norsk Sjorfartsmuseum

BRONWEN

Type: Sailing Vessel, 3 Masted Schooner
Port of Registry: London
Built: 1891
Date of Sinking: September 21st 1891
Location: Quarry Head, New Quay, Dyfed

The BRONWEN was a spanking new three masted schooner, owned by Richards of Porthmadog but she failed to survive her first voyage. She was wrecked at New Quay in 1891, the same year that she was built.

The BRONWEN had left the Ayrshire port of Ardrosson on Saturday night 19th September 1891, intending to sail south for Cadiz to load her first cargo for an Atlantic crossing to Rio Grande. Unfortunately, by Sunday morning, a severe rainstorm swept over North Wales and made conditions rough in the Irish Sea, the barometer continued to fall and several towns near Edinburgh suffered severe flooding. The worst storm of a very wet autumn had arrived and the BRONWEN was driven headlong in front of a strong north westerly wind to arrive on the Dyfed coast out of control.

It was a Monday evening when the BRONWEN drove on to the rocky beach below the sheer cliffs at Quarry Head, just outside New Quay. When the people of New Quay heard the news they rushed out of the town to see the wreck as it came pounding ashore. The BRONWEN crashed on to the beach and her hull was shaken violently and persistently as each wave hit her. Ropes were thrown by the schooner's crew down to the local men on the beach who had gathered to help. The ropes were quickly rigged up to make an escape route for those aboard. The BRONWEN'S new iron built hull stayed intact long enough for all the crew and the Captain's wife to get ashore. By the time the Rocket Brigade arrived at the scene their equipment was not needed as all on board had already come safely ashore.

The survivors were taken care of by the local agent of the Shipwrecked Mariners' Society, and within a few days the BRONWEN became a total wreck. It was sad to see the end of schooner that was so new that she had not taken aboard her first cargo. Some artefacts from the wrecked BRONWEN, the centre boss of the ship's wheel and her nameboard, are still to be seen in New Quay today.

Carved nameboard from the BRONWEN.

It was unusual for a Porthmadoc owner to order an iron built schooner. The BRONWEN was one such vessel but she was wrecked on her maiden voyage

Photo: New Quay Town Council

CALBURGA

Type: Sailing Vessel, 3 Masted Barque
Port of Registry: Halifax, Nova Scotia
Official Number: 90478
Tonnage: 1,406 tons gross
Built: 1890, South Maitland, Nova Scotia
Length: 210 feet
Breadth: 39 feet
Date of Sinking: November 13th 1915
Location: Near Strumble Head, Pembrokeshire, Dyfed

A November gale in 1915 saw the wrecking of two large barques off the West Wales coast, fortunately both crews survived. These two ships were amongst the last square rigged sailing ships to be lost in the area and it signified the passing of the era of sail. Both vessels were large 3 masted barques and both had a Canadian timber cargo intended for Liverpool.

A hurricane blew from the north east for fourteen hours. The strong wind caused the FORMOSA to be caught inside the Middle Bishops where she hit one of the many submerged rocks. Her crew escaped into two of the ship's longboats, one boat was found by the St David's Lifeboat and the other came in at Whitesands, where it overturned in the surf and all 7 men had to swim ashore.

The saving of the crew of the other barque, the CALBURGA, was no less dramatic. With all the barque's sails blown out and two of her three masts fallen, the ship was at the mercy of the wind. Captain W D Nelson took the decision to abandon before they hit the high cliffs near Strumble Head. All 14 men took to one ship's boat and with their Captain at the helm they rowed through the big seas to look for a place to land. Seeing the coastline dip near St Nicholas they made for Aberbach where, with great seamanship, they surfed the boat onto the beach, Captain Nelson, standing at the stern, skillfully directing the lifeboat through the waves with a long steering oar. While they were coming ashore the CALBURGA lodged herself on the rocks at Penbrush Point and the Fishguard

Lifeboat later arrived but finding no one assumed the crew had all drowned.

The CALBURGA had left her home port of Halifax a month before and had taken 18 days to cross the Atlantic to reach the Fastnets. They then met with continuous gales and for 9 days struggled to proceed beyond Tuskar Rock in heavy easterly squalls. A north east gale hit them and, before they could be lowered, the main topsails were blown clean out of the ropes. Heavy seas were shipped, pounding the deck cargo and making the barque waterlogged. By nightfall the deck cargo on the starboard side had washed away and the gale increased to hurricane force shredding every yard of canvas. The cabin was completely smashed by falling timber and the seas rushed in pinning the Steward underwater. He was saved from drowning in the nick of time by Captain Nelson.

The CALBURGA hit the shore head on, her hull pivoted on two underwater rocks which broke her back and caused her to spill her timber cargo. A few hours later a large section of her hull was taken a little way with the tide before finally sinking into the deep water next to the cliffs.

The ship provided a veritable bonanza of timber. It was reported that there was so much timber that you could walk out over the sea on it without getting your feet wet. The local farmers were kept busy for weeks carting the planks of deal up the cliffs using haymaking poles, pullies and the farm horses.

The author has a particular fascination for this ship as it was one of the first he personally located underwater in 1975. Although the main part of the wreckage lies at 43 metres, there are bits of iron, a large anchor and anchor chain at a shallow depth and provided you respect the strong currents these make an interesting dive.

The Maritime Museum of the Atlantic in Halifax, Nova Scotia has a superb 51 inch replica model of the CALBURGA. She was the last of the square riggers to trade from this Canadian port and when visiting the Museum in 1982, I was fortunate to see the model when it had just been completed. (See the photograph page 112).

Inset photo shows fid, belaying pins, pulley and door recovered from the barque when she was lost in 1915

Canadian barque CALBURGA at Parrsboro River, Nova Scotia
Photo: Maritime Museum of the Atlantic, Nova Scotia

How to locate the CALBURGA

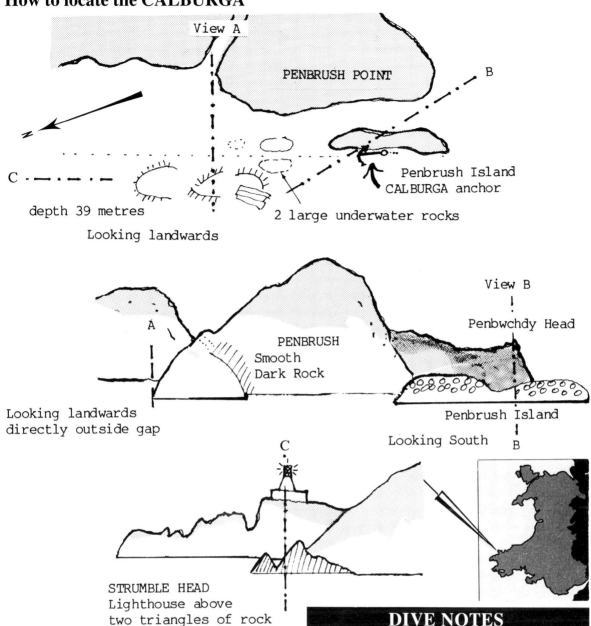

View A

PENBRUSH POINT

B

C

Penbrush Island
CALBURGA anchor

depth 39 metres

2 large underwater rocks

Looking landwards

View B

Penbwchdy Head

PENBRUSH
Smooth
Dark Rock

A

Looking landwards
directly outside gap

Penbrush Island

Looking South

C

STRUMBLE HEAD
Lighthouse above
two triangles of rock

DIVE DETAILS

Location: 52° 01'04" N   05° 05'35" W
About 80 metres North West of Penbrush Point
Depth: 35m to 43m (Anchor in shallows at 12m)
Seabed: rock & shingle, some silt
Currents: strong, 3 knots,
Underwater Visibility: usually good
Launch Site: Porthgain, Abercastle or
 Goodwick, Fishguard

DIVE NOTES

This is a dive that requires planning and slack
water. There seem to be two slacks each tide.
Slack water generally 1½ to 2 hrs after Low and
High Water Milford Haven.
If you did not wish to go deep but seeking a
worthwhile dive - descend at north end of
Penbrush Island and travel southward along the
outer edge of the islet at about 12 metres. You
will see the CALBURGA Admiralty pattern
anchor (3½ metre shank) and one of the prettiest
rocks in the area.

CAMBRO

Type: Cargo Steamship
Port of Registry: Cardiff
Tonnage: 1,918 tons
Built: 1906, Campeltown
Length: 282 feet
Breadth: 40 feet
Engines: Triple Expansion, 192 nhp
Date of Sinking: May 24th 1913
Location: Smalls, Pembrokeshire, Dyfed

A dense fog prevailed as Captain Rich commanded the CAMBRO on a northerly course for the last part of a voyage from Huelva, Spain to Garston in Lancashire. The steamer was heavily laden with a cargo of iron-ore and carrying a compliment of 20 men. The entire Pembrokeshire coastline was covered in a thick fog when, with a mighty thud, the steamer struck the Smalls rocks.

The CAMBRO struck the rocks just as it was getting dark, two hours before high water. As the tide rose the steamer stuck fast and

The CAMBRO sinking, the Smalls lighthouse beyond
Photo: Trevor Owens Collection

rapidly filled. The unlucky crew found themselves in a very remote position, some 16 miles from the mainland. The decision was taken to abandon the ship. Launching two of the ship's lifeboats, half the crew went in one boat under the command of the Second Officer and the remainder boarded the other boat under Captain Rich. Both lifeboats pulled away from the sunken steamer but they soon lost sight of each other in the fog and the darkness.

The Second Officer had with him the First, Second and Third Engineers, a sailor, 4 Firemen and the mess room Steward. It was not long before they were spotted by a passing steamer.

The steamer OPAL, on her way to London, took these men on board and later landed them at Weymouth. A Lloyd's message from Portland reported that they had been picked up.

Captain Rich, in the other lifeboat, was determined not to rely solely on passing steamers for help and in grand style he encouraged the men in his boat to row throughout the night in the direction of Milford Haven. In the early hours the fog lifted and after rowing at least 21 miles across the tidal streams for eleven hours they all arrived safely at the port of Milford Haven, a truly astonishing feat. As they arrived news was reaching the port that their vessel had sunk.

How to locate the CAMBRO

(Divers are asked to check if the 'Smalls Wreck', Restricted Area applies to this site)

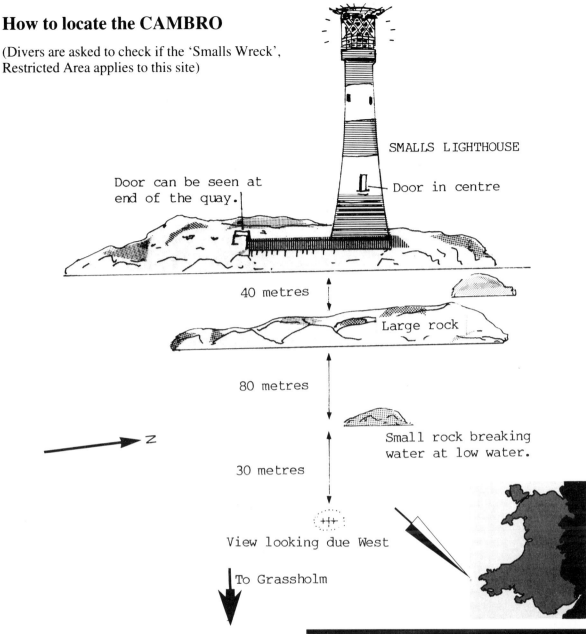

SMALLS LIGHTHOUSE

Door can be seen at end of the quay.

Door in centre

40 metres

Large rock

80 metres

Small rock breaking water at low water.

30 metres

N

View looking due West

To Grassholm

DIVE DETAILS

Location: 51° 43'07" N 05° 40'10" W
About 150 metres due East of Smalls Lighthouse
Depth: 12m to 22m
Seabed: rock & shingle
Currents: up to 3 knots
Underwater Visibility: very good
Launch Site: Gelliswick, Milford Haven
          Porthclais or Broadhaven

DIVE NOTES

The Smalls is remote; it takes over an hour to get there by fast inflatable, and should only be visited in settled weather with well equipped boats, preferably in tandem, and always with a radiotelephone. There is always somewhere to dive throughout the day in the shelter of the strong tides.
Slack water at the Smalls is 1 hour before H.W. Milford Haven and 5 hours after H.W. Milford Haven.

CHARLES HOLMES

Type: Sailing Vessel, Square Rigged Ship
Port of Registry: Liverpool (?)
Tonnage: 886 tons
Built: 1852, North America
Date of Sinking: October 25th 1859
Location: Aberbach, Pembrokeshire, Dyfed

The two days of gale which wrecked the ROYAL CHARTER in October 1859 caused a phenomenal amount of suffering, loss of life and shipwreck around the entire Welsh coastline. In the forty miles of coastline between Cardigan and St David's Head no less than nine ships were wrecked and a total of 40 lives were lost, an average of one life lost per mile of coast. Some of the ships were lost with their entire crew and such was the situation with the CHARLES HOLMES.

The churchyard at Granston has a gravestone which reads 'In memory of Captain C. H. N. Bowlby and the crew of ship CHARLES HOLMES, lost with all hands at Aberbach'. It was generally thought by the local people to be an emigrant ship by the mixed cargo that was being carried but a telegram from Liverpool four days after the tragedy confirmed that there were no emigrants on board.

The ship was sailing outward from Liverpool to start an Atlantic crossing to Mobile, near New Orleans. The cargo consisted of general goods intended to make life more comfortable for the settlers in that part of America. Deep in the hold was a cargo of iron and elsewhere the mixed cargo of meat, clothing, tools including pocket-knives and an assortment of new crockery.

Fully laden she was making her course southward when one of the most ferocious storms of the last century hit her. She was driven towards the Pembrokeshire cliffs and at the last minute one can only imagine that her Captain attempted to beach her at either Abermawr or Aberbach. The wind strength and seas were so strong that they were hurled into a small cove named Porth Dwgan where the ship grounded on an underwater pinnacle and prompty capsized. Although the cliffs are scaleable under normal circumstances, not one of the crew survived and most of the bodies that were recovered were found in a large cave at the rear of the cove.

The first reports of the wreck stated that she was bottom up and a mass of wreck. A report three days later gave the information that a quantity of wreckage was at both Aberbach and at Abermawr and that 5 bodies had been picked up, the sea was still running too high to take off the rest.

The newspaper failed to report the most interesting story of all which has become local knowledge during this century. A young farm lad spotted a locked chest amongst the ship's wreckage. He picked it up and was taking it home when a local farmer stopped him and gave him a shilling for it before sending the boy on his way. That evening the chinking sound of coins caused an inquisitive servant girl to peep through the floorboards into the farmhouse kitchen below. What she saw made her eyes pop out for there below was the farmer with a chest full of golden sovereigns. The local people subsequently noticed a distinct improvement in the prosperity of the farmer.

The ship owners were keen to employ the services of a diver on the wreck and the already retrieved riches may have been their objective. In May the following year they managed to get a well known diver Captain Hicks from Falmouth to start diving operations. The local newspaper reported, 'he has been very successful so far, without having the unpleasant sensation of going under water to work. A quantity of iron has already been shipped for Liverpool, and if the weather continues fine the greater part of the cargo will be secured in the month'.

In 1976 the author carried out an intensive search of the seabed (just in case there was a second gold chest waiting on the seabed for him to pick up!). No coins were found but there are thousands of pottery pieces, small broken pieces of cups, plates, dishes, bowls and the like. Some have the ceramic mark of Morley & Ashworth, a partnership of potters at Hanley, Stoke-on-Trent in the years 1858 to 1862, which coincide with the date of the wreck.

Barque similar to CHARLES HOLMES crashing into rocks
Photo: Illustrated London News

Gravestone to the captain and crew
Photo: Tom Bennett

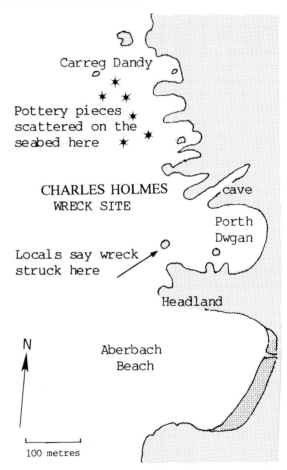

Carreg Dandy

Pottery pieces scattered on the seabed here

CHARLES HOLMES
WRECK SITE

cave

Porth
Dwgan

Locals say wreck struck here

Headland

N

Aberbach
Beach

100 metres

DIVE DETAILS

Location: 51° 58'27"N 05° 05'10"W
Depth: 6m to 9m
Seabed: gravel, boulders & weed
Currents: negligible
Underwater Visibility: good
Launch Site: Abercastle, Porthgain or Goodwick

COUNT D'ASPREMONT

Type: Cargo Steamship
Port of Registry: Swansea
Official Number: 70222
Previous Name: OTHELLO
Tonnage: 452 tons gross
Built: 1874, Newcastle
Length: 163 feet
Breadth: 23 feet
Date of Sinking: December 9th 1903
Location: Ramsey Sound, Pembrokeshire, Dyfed

The COUNT D'ASPREMONT was in many ways typical of the coastal steamships that were working around our coastline a century ago. Iron built by the shipbuilders C.S.Swan & Company in Newcastle, 452 tons gross (274 tons net), she was first registered on completion of her building in 1874. Her first owner was G.Reid of Newcastle but the following year she was sold to L.Balgeurie and Sons of Rotterdam and her name changed to OTHELLO. She was reregistered in Swansea in 1892 when her name was changed back to COUNT D'ASPREMONT. For a time she was owned by Thomas Harries, shipbroker, 23 Bryn Road, Swansea and in 1898 she was bought by the Anglo American Agency Co. Ltd of 33 Mount Stuart Square, Cardiff.

Like many contemporary steamships, her stern shape was described as 'elliptical' and her straight stemmed bow as 'vertical'. She had just one deck and was schooner rigged with two masts. The sails would have been rarely used but were carried in case of engine failure.

Her engines were two compound steam engines each developing 65 nhp, built by Christie Gutch and Company of Newcastle and after eleven years use she required two new boilers.

Like the majority of steamers of her day her loss was technically referred to as 'a stranding', which usually meant hitting the coastline. In the case of the COUNT D'ASPREMONT it was hitting Horse Rock in the middle of the boisterous waters of Ramsey Sound.

The Shipping Gazette reported as follows; 'St David's, December 9th, 6pm. Steamer COUNT D'ASPREMONT of Swansea, Captain Wood, from Dublin for Newport in ballast; fast ashore on Horse Rock, Ramsey Sound, likely become total wreck. Crew saved in their own boat.'

Four hours later the stranded steamer was taken off the rock by the north going tide and foundered 300 metres away, about midway between the rock and the Lifeboat slipway at St Justinian.

Diver friends of mine located wreckage in Ramsey Sound in 1982 and asked me what steamer it might be. Searching my files I realized that it could be one of three wrecks and suggested that it would be helpful if a beam measurement could be taken to help with the identification. A few days later they took me to the spot and I dived down taking a tape measure with me. The beam measured about 22 feet which was similar to two steamers lost near Horse Rock. We still could not be sure of her identity until a stroke of luck the following weekend when we revisited. One of our team came across the ship builder's brass plate and the building date of 1874 clearly marked on it. This was the confirmation we were looking for, the wreck of the COUNT D'ASPREMONT had been found.

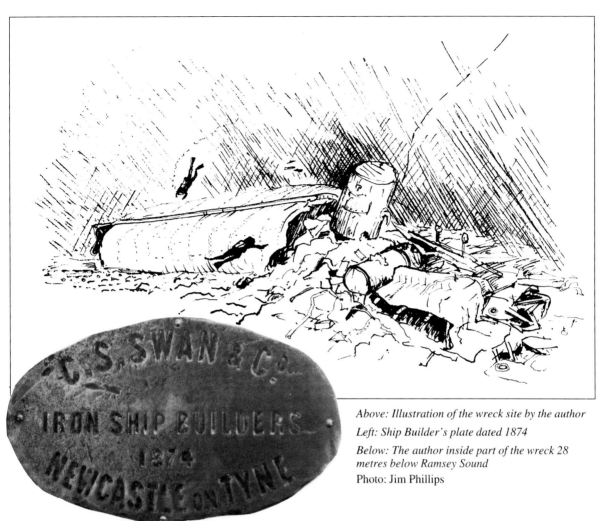

Above: Illustration of the wreck site by the author

Left: Ship Builder's plate dated 1874

Below: The author inside part of the wreck 28 metres below Ramsey Sound

Photo: Jim Phillips

DIVE DETAILS

Location: 05° 18'58" N 51° 52'25" W
About 300 metres North West of Horse Rock,
Ramsey Sound
Depth: 28m
Seabed: rock & small stones
Currents: strong, 5 knots.
Underwater Visibility: good
Launch Site: Porthclais or Porthgain

DIVE NOTES

The turbulent waters of Ramsey Sound should be
treated with respect, this is a slack water dive.
The safer slack is the one 2 hours 10 minutes after
Low Water Milford Haven, as the northgoing
tidal stream commences.

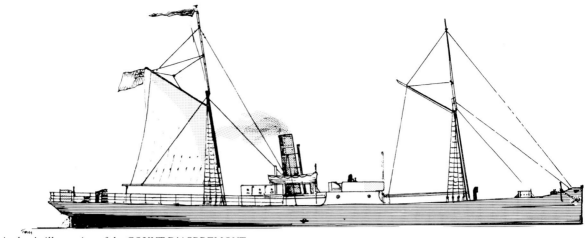

Author's illustration of the COUNT D'ASPREMONT

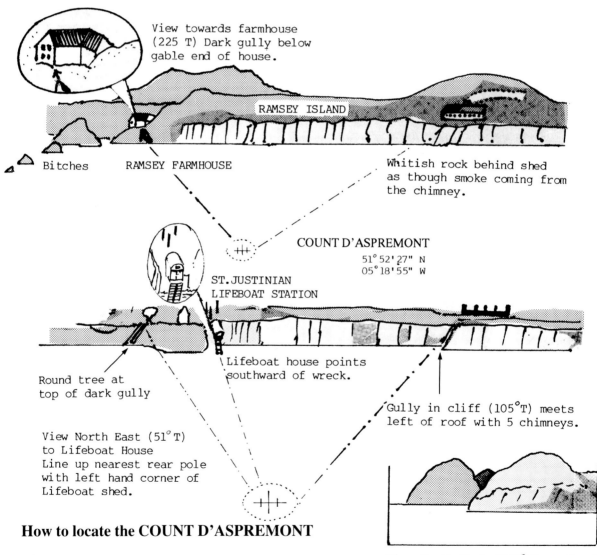

View towards farmhouse
(225 T) Dark gully below
gable end of house.

RAMSEY ISLAND

Bitches   RAMSEY FARMHOUSE

Whitish rock behind shed
as though smoke coming from
the chimney.

COUNT D'ASPREMONT

51°52'27" N
05°18'55" W

ST.JUSTINIAN
LIFEBOAT STATION

Round tree at
top of dark gully

Lifeboat house points
southward of wreck.

Gully in cliff (105°T) meets
left of roof with 5 chimneys.

View North East (51°T)
to Lifeboat House
Line up nearest rear pole
with left hand corner of
Lifeboat shed.

How to locate the COUNT D'ASPREMONT

View South West (205°T) at South
end of Ramsey, Ynys Bery behind.

CRESSWELL

Type: Sailing Ship, Barque Rigged
Port of Registry: Sunderland
Official Number: 47650
Tonnage: 464 tons
Built: 1863, Sunderland
Length: 140 feet
Breadth: 28 feet
Date of Sinking: January 27th 1881
Location: Paviland Cliffs, Gower, Glamorgan

The Sunderland barque CRESSWELL was sailing south from Liverpool to Cardiff in ballast when she went severely off course. Her Master, Captain W.Cruse could not blame his actions on the state of the weather as it was only wind force three from the south-east, nevertheless his ship sailed over the Helwick Shoal and struck the rocks under Paviland Cliffs at 9.30 am on a January morning in 1881, it was nearing low tide.

The Captain decided to take his wife to the safety of the land, so with the help of three crew members they launched one of the ship's boats and rowed ashore.

A group of Porteynon men were quick to hear that a sailing ship had stranded nearby, and six of them launched a boat and rowed out to the CRESSWELL, where they found 9 men on board. The Porteynon boat offered to take the men ashore, and 4 gladly accepted, the other 5 refused to leave unless they could take their chests of belongings with them. This somewhat infuriated the rescuers as their boat was not big enough to take the chests aswell and they replied 'We are come to save life, not property!'

There were still two ship's boats on the CRESSWELL, one on the deck and one in her davits; the Porteynon men decided to leave. An observer on land, seeing a boat leave the ship assumed that all the crew had left, and reported this to the Coastguard. The Coastguard investigated and saw, to his surprise, some of the crew still on board. He summoned the Rhossili Rocket Crew to help with a rescue.

Richard Bevan, one of the Porteynon rescuers, was critical that the anchors of the CRESSWELL had not been released when she stranded. He wrote in the Cambrian newspaper; 'The men that remained on board appeared to think that the ship would hold together that tide, and no doubt she would have done so if, when she first struck the ground, her anchors had been let go; they would have kept her head to sea so that she would have been driven in on the flood tide end on and have held together one or two tides, and all her stores, spare canvas and other materials could have been saved. By being left to take her chance she drove in broadside and parted amidships shortly after high water, when from the steepness of the rocks and the ebb tide settling down and off, nearly all the things were carried out to sea.'

Mr Bevan was not the only one critical of the Captain, the Board of Trade later concluded that the Master was in default for steering an improper course and for navigating in an unseamanlike manner.

The rocket apparatus was set up on the cliff about two hours after the Porteynon boat had left the ship. The first rocket was accurately fired over the ship which was already starting to break up. The men were rescued by breeches buoy, without their sea chests, and ten minutes after the last crewman was rescued the CRESSWELL completely broke up.

DALSERF

Type: Cargo Steamship
Port of Registry: Glasgow
Tonnage: 1,849 tons gross
Built: 1909, Stockton on Tees
Length: 260 feet
Breadth: 40 feet
Engines: 209 nhp
Date of Sinking: July 10th 1910
Location: Grassholm Island, Pembrokeshire, Dyfed

It was mid summer in 1910 when the Glasgow steamer DALSERF was on a voyage from Penarth to Oban with a cargo of coal. A sea fog enveloped the steamer when she was off the Pembrokeshire coast and her Master was forced to reassess his position. Unfortunately, in making his navigational calculations he placed too much reliance upon his distance off St Govan's Lightship. It was unfortunate because the distance was incorrect. He had also underestimated his distance from St Ann's Head. His navigational errors caused his vessel to hit the rocks at Grassholm Island, some 9 miles off the mainland. The DALSERF became holed and grounded in nine metres of water.

An attempt was made to refloat her, an ambitious scheme, utterly reliant on the weather, but being mid summer it was worth a try. Lloyd's Weekly Shipping Index records the day by day struggle of the unsuccessful salvage attempt.

Work started on July 13th under the Salvage Association's Cardiff Surveyor. The first job was to jettison the coal cargo and it was expected to discharge about 1,300 tons before attempting to refloat her. Weather was fine when they started and five days later he reported, 'Tried pump in engine room again, reduced water 7 feet per hour, petrol pumps left on board. Hope try

after-hold tomorrow. Am fitting 12 inch pump in forehold, work proceeding satisfactory'.

The photographs were taken about this time and then the weather deteriorated and no work could be carried out. On July 28th the salvage team went out to the island hoping to work but there was too much sea to board the wreck, the Surveyor left his assistant and a ten man team to camp on the island.

On August 2nd a heavy easterly gale took away two boats that were moored alongside the DALSERF but apart from giving her a greater list to port the storm did no further damage to her hull. Six days later the team had stopped up a leak in the engine room and had pumped her out to just afloat. With the weather wet but all well and a smooth sea, the men only needed to trim the remaining cargo before the big float. The weather beat them again but they continued on August 18th with 'Diver worked two hours at low water but was unable to continue owing to heavy swell'. Two days later a strong east southeasterly smashed into the wreck and it broke into five pieces, taking the funnel and bridge structure away completely. On August 22nd the Salvage Association announced that the DALSERF was a total loss.

Extensive pumping and salvage operations during the 1910 summer failed to refloat the DALSERF
Photo: Trevor Owens Collection

The DALSERF breaking up on Grassholm
Photo: Trevor Owens Collection

DIVE DETAILS

Location: 51° 43'44" N   05° 28'32" W
About 150 metres South of East Tump, Grassholm
Depth: 17m to 23m
Seabed: rock & small stones
Currents: up to 4½ knots
Underwater Visibility: good
Launch Site:

from Martin's Haven	9 nautical miles
from Porthclais	11 nautical miles
from Whitesands	12 nautical miles
from Broadhaven	14 nautical miles
from Dale	15 nautical miles
from Porthgain	18 nautical miles

DIVE NOTES

The journey to Grassholm will take about 50 minutes by inflatable from Porthclais. Grassholm is a bird sanctuary for gannets and landing is forbidden. Interesting dives can be made all around the island in depths ranging from 16 to 40 metres. Take a VHF radiotelephone and only go in calm weather, avoid spring tides which might impair the underwater visibility.
Slack Water 1 hour 35 minutes before and 4 hours 40 minutes after H.W. Milford Haven.

Winch parts and anchor of
Sailing vessel close to cliff,
possibly ELLEN lost 1893

Gannet Colony
(15,000 pairs)
on this side of island

Grassholm
Island

East Tump

150 metres

N

DALSERF
51°43'44"N 05°28'32"W

EL TAMBO

Type: Cattle Freighter
Port of Registry: Panama
Previous Names: CORINTHIAN, MARIA RUSS.
Tonnage: 1,241 tons gross
Built: 1961, Rendsburg
Length: 93 metres
Breadth: 12 metres
Date of Sinking: March 27th 1977
Location: Fishguard Harbour, Pembrokeshire, Dyfed

It was blowing a force nine on a cold March Sunday afternoon when the author happened to be sitting in his car overlooking Fishguard Harbour. A companion shouted urgently 'Hey, look,' he was pointing to the EL TAMBO a freighter that had been moored in the harbour for six weeks following a fire on board. 'Its moving,' he explained. I looked and sure enough the ship's list which had been prominent for a few weeks was increasing visibly by the minute. 'Let's call the Coastguard,' he offered. 'You can call them,' I replied, 'I am staying here, I don't think there's anyone aboard and I haven't seen a ship sink before!'

My companion, who was a member of the Lifeboat crew, duly vanished to the Coastguard's house and then to the Lifeboat while I collected a

Cattleship EL TAMBO lying submerged at Fishguard. She remained like this from March 1977 to August 1980
Photo: Tom Bennett

camera and watched the whole scene from the cliff top. Sure enough, the EL TAMBO keeled over on her side and then her bow sank until it hit the seabed. She was in ten metres of water and her stern stayed afloat for the next few hours. I was wrong about nobody being aboard. There was one watchman aboard, an Italian, who was thrown out of his bunk when the ship listed and he escaped just as the decks were awash. Bales of straw floated out of her hold and the man started climbing on top of them, waving his arms frantically for help as he was washed away from the wreck. The Fishguard Lifeboat was soon there to pick him out of the water and within ten minutes he was transferred to a RAF Helicopter and taken to Haverfordwest Hospital.

The EL TAMBO saga started some six weeks before this and continued for another three years. In February 1977 the EL TAMBO, with a cargo of 917 cattle from Ireland, developed engine trouble in the Irish Sea and made for Fishguard for repairs. After five days she resumed her journey to take the cattle to Libyan slaughterhouses but had only gone 10 miles when a fire broke out. All 21 crew members were safely taken off the blazing vessel by lifeboats from the Ro-Ro ferry AVALON, and

the fire was put out by the combined teams of a number of vessels which responded to the distress. A Navy survey ship towed the stricken ship into Fishguard Harbour. The cattle were marooned on board until the RSPCA complained of poor conditions. It was national news and the Prime Minister, Mr Jim Callaghan, intervened after seeing the animals' plight on the television. A Minister was sent down to inspect but two Dutch cattle carriers, summoned by the cattle owners, arrived to rescue the animals at the same time. The cattle were transferred on February 13th to the two Dutch ships and the bullocks resumed their journey.

The Admiralty Marshal placed the freighter under arrest while salvage claims were made and the legal tangle became more complex the day the EL TAMBO sank. The semi submerged wreck caused something of an obstruction for the ferry traffic. Because she lay half submerged the task of lifting her complete was made more difficult, hampered by severe weather and the fact that she became embedded in 4 metres of mud. The wreck was eventually removed three years later by being cut up underwater, transported ashore in five large pieces and then cut up for scrap.

Superstructure of EL TAMBO ashore prior to being taken to the scrapyard
Photo: David Owen

FELLSIDE

Type: Cargo Steamship
Port of Registry: Cardiff
Official Number: 11037
Tonnage: 872 tons
Built: 1901, Port Glasgow
Length: 209 feet
Breadth: 30 feet
Engines: 114 nhp
Date of Sinking: January 8th 1924
Location: Heatherslade Bay, Gower, Glamorgan

A Telegram from Oxwich on January 8th 1924 broke the news to the insurers, it read, 'Steamer FELLSIDE, on rocks at Three Cliffs, is likely to become a total wreck. Crew landed here; one man drowned'.

The Cardiff steamer was bound for Swansea with a cargo of pit-props when she encountered severe weather off the Gower coast and at 5.00am during a dense fog she was driven onto the rocks in Hunts Bay, Heatherslade, south of Southgate.

Two Coastguards on duty at Oxwich were first alerted to the wreck by the arrival of one of the crew in an open boat. They immediately contacted the Mumbles Lifeboat. During this time the FELLSIDE's Master, Captain S. E. Drake, a Cardiff man, decided that the crew should leave the wreck and the ship's own lifeboats were lowered over the side. By the time the Mumbles Lifeboat arrived her services were not required. When the first lifeboat was leaving the ship's side one of the crew fell into the swirling water and was drowned. The body of J. P. O'Brien, a native of Birmingham, was never found.

The steamer received a severe buffeting on the rocks but the officers and crew escaped taking with them their personal belongings. Captain Drake and the First Officer remained on board while the boats made their way to Oxwich where 13 crewmen were greeted by the villagers who rushed down to the beach to help.

During the next night there was a severe storm, the full effect of which hit the wrecked steamer and the Captain and First Officer were forced to go ashore. As the tide rose the sea beat against the hull and washed clean over the vessel, taking with it some of the deck cargo of pit-props. The photograph shows the pit-prop cargo in disarray on her decks.

This storm, described as a terrific blizzard, caused extensive damage to shipping including the French schooner ADOLPH which sank off Nash Sands with the loss of her Captain.

The FELLSIDE, as the original telegram had implied, did become a total wreck, and was purchased by the local firm, H. Greening & Sons of Killay, who cut her up for scrap.

The Cardiff steamer FELLSIDE ran into the rocks of Heatherslade Bay, Gower in a fog in 1924. Her cargo of pit-props can be seen in disarray on her decks

Photo: Bryan Andrews of Kelpies

FORT MEDINE

Type: Cargo Steamship
Port of Registry: Swansea
Official Number: 140857
Previous Name: BRADFORD CITY
Tonnage: 5,335 tons gross
Built: 1919, Stockton on Tees
Date of Sinking: February 20th 1941
Location: Off Mumbles Head, Swansea, Glamorgan

On February 20th 1941 the Mumbles Lifeboat went out to a large cargo vessel that had been blown up by an enemy mine. The ship was the FORT MEDINE. She sank only four miles away from Swansea, her home port. Swansea had an air raid lasting three consecutive nights during the same week.

The FORT MEDINE sank immediately with the devastation caused by the explosion. When the Mumbles Lifeboat, EDWARD, PRINCE OF WALES, arrived at the scene only oil and some floating wreckage could be seen on the water. Fortunately, some of the crew had abandoned the sinking ship into two ship's lifeboats, and a pilot cutter had reached the spot before the Lifeboat. The pilot cutter had already picked up these men before the Lifeboat arrived and although a thorough search was made of the water they failed to find any other survivors. The two lifeboats were towed back to Mumbles pier by the Lifeboat.

The FORT MEDINE was steel built in 1919 and had been formerly named BRADFORD CITY and also FORT MEDINE of France.

DIVE DETAILS

Location: 51° 33'22" N 03° 56'15" W
Depth: 18m to 20m
Seabed: sand
Currents: 2 knots
Underwater Visibility: very poor
Launch Site: Mumbles

Note: Protection of Military Remains Act 1986 may apply. Little diving information is known but the wreckage is understood to be severely flattened with steel plates rising about two metres above the seabed.

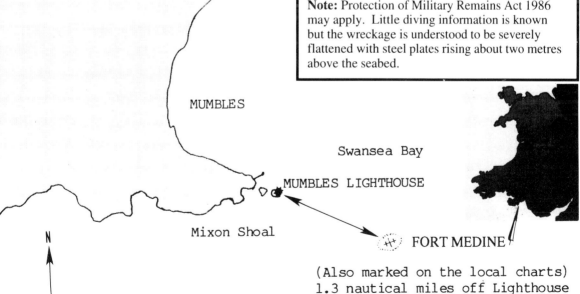

(Also marked on the local charts)
1.3 nautical miles off Lighthouse

GILBERT THOMPSON

Type: Sailing Vessel, Barque Rigged
Port of Registry: Liverpool
Official Number: 44688
Tonnage: 1,061 tons gross
Built: 1862, Birkenhead
Length: 187 feet
Breadth: 34 feet
Date of Sinking: March 5th 1881
Location: West Mouse, Anglesey, Gwynedd

The GILBERT THOMPSON was iron built by Laird and Sons at Birkenhead in 1862. Built as a fully rigged ship she was registered as a barque from 1879. The Liverpool firm of Edward Bates & Son managed the ship for her entire nineteen years until she was lost off the north coast of Anglesey in 1881.

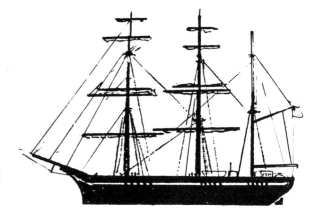

The GILBERT THOMPSON was completing a long voyage from Calcutta to her home port, and was under tow with a tug. They were negotiating the notorious channel between the Skerries and the West Mouse Rock when she slightly moved over to starboard, and thudded to a halt. On board was a compliment of 22, commanded by Captain Vincent. The ship lurched and fell over with the strong tide, her iron hull torn apart on the underwater reef to the west of the West Mouse Rock. Frantically, the orders were given to abandon the ship and 21 crew managed to scramble from the ship onto the rocks as the vessel slid into the water.

All escaped from the ship except for one, a cabin boy who was lying in his bunk when the ship went down. Because he was disabled with a broken leg he could not escape from the sinking ship fast enough. The crew were taken off the rock by the tug and taken to Liverpool.

The GILBERT THOMPSON was carrying a general cargo from Calcutta and the Liverpool Salvage Association reported the next day that the ship was lying broadside with her yardarms showing at half ebb and with five fathoms of water alongside her.

How to locate the GILBERT THOMPSON

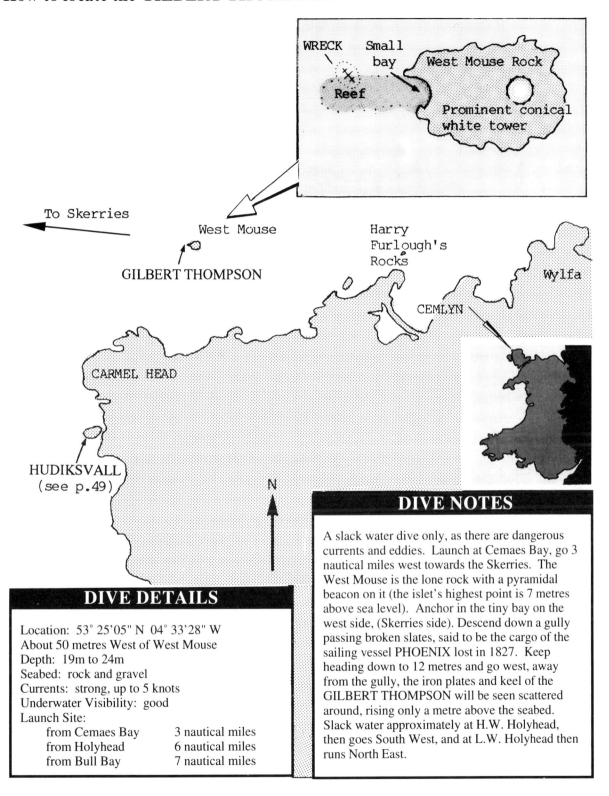

WRECK   Small bay

Reef

West Mouse Rock

Prominent conical white tower

To Skerries

West Mouse

GILBERT THOMPSON

Harry Furlough's Rocks

Wylfa

CEMLYN

CARMEL HEAD

HUDIKSVALL (see p.49)

N

DIVE DETAILS

Location: 53° 25'05" N 04° 33'28" W
About 50 metres West of West Mouse
Depth: 19m to 24m
Seabed: rock and gravel
Currents: strong, up to 5 knots
Underwater Visibility: good
Launch Site:

from Cemaes Bay	3 nautical miles
from Holyhead	6 nautical miles
from Bull Bay	7 nautical miles

DIVE NOTES

A slack water dive only, as there are dangerous currents and eddies. Launch at Cemaes Bay, go 3 nautical miles west towards the Skerries. The West Mouse is the lone rock with a pyramidal beacon on it (the islet's highest point is 7 metres above sea level). Anchor in the tiny bay on the west side, (Skerries side). Descend down a gully passing broken slates, said to be the cargo of the sailing vessel PHOENIX lost in 1827. Keep heading down to 12 metres and go west, away from the gully, the iron plates and keel of the GILBERT THOMPSON will be seen scattered around, rising only a metre above the seabed. Slack water approximately at H.W. Holyhead, then goes South West, and at L.W. Holyhead then runs North East.

GLENISLA

Type: Cargo Steamship
Port of Registry: Leith
Official Number: 87260
Tonnage: 1,283 tons gross
Built: 1883, Newcastle
Length: 265 feet
Breadth: 36 feet
Engines: Compound 2 cylinder, 160 nhp
Date of Sinking: February 28th 1886
Location: Abereiddy, Pembrokeshire, Dyfed

Laden with 1,885 tons of coal the steamer GLENISLA was bound for a port in Italy when a simple error in identifying a lighthouse caused her loss on a reef off the Pembrokeshire coast in 1886. The weather was good when her Captain, Allan Wallace, was in command of the GLENISLA as she steamed in a southerly direction from Glasgow. For this trip to Savona in the Gulf of Genoa, Captain Wallace was

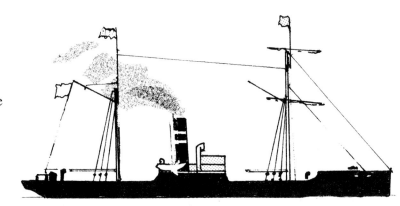

taking his wife with him, but their voyage was short. He made the mistake of altering his course after seeing, but not properly identifying, a lighthouse. As he approached the coast near St David's he saw the South Bishop Light but mistook it for a light off the Irish coast.

The light that was actually seen in the dark that Sunday morning at 3.30am was the white light revolving every 20 seconds of The South Bishops. (Today this light is a Flash every 5 seconds). Captain Wallace probably thought it was the Arklow Bank South, a lightship that gave a white revolving light every 30 seconds. This caused him to think he was too near to the Irish coast and he altered course to the south assuming that he was steaming in the middle of St George's Channel. His new course was a big mistake as his ship was now heading straight for St David's Head. At 4am, with the GLENISLA steaming at full speed she hit an underwater reef about half a mile from the shore. All 21 crewmen, the Captain and his wife took to the

ship's lifeboats. The sea was reasonably calm and the boats remained in the vicinity of the wreck throughout the cold night. When daylight came they were astonished to see that they were close to land and quickly rowed the half mile to Aberpwll, a beach close to Abereiddy.

The Leith steamer had run over the rock with such a force that she had ended up straddled across it. The swell soon broke the back of the heavily laden ship and her stern half slipped beneath the waves, leaving the fo'castle and middle sections pierced on top of the reef. The crewmen lost all their possessions, but were lucky to get safely ashore without any injuries; two days later they were returning to their homes.

In 1983 a diver friend of mine informed me that The Pembrokeshire Herald in 1886 had an article about the GLENISLA loss mentioning Llech Ganol rock as the place of sinking. Having dived many times near that rock and not seen steamer wreckage, a small group of us decided to do a thorough search. On compass courses radiating out from the rock it took only an hour to locate the wreckage. The ship, as expected, after a century below the waves, was completely broken up, with much of her coal cargo interspersed amongst the iron plates and embedded amongst broken parts of the wooden superstructure. The photographs show some of the artifacts recovered including cutlery bearing the ship's name, a useful confirmation of the true identity of this wreck.

Compass plate, porthole and fork recovered from the wreck.

The ship's name on the cutlery identified the wreck site.

Ship's wheel boss showing the name GLENISLA.

How to locate the GLENISLA

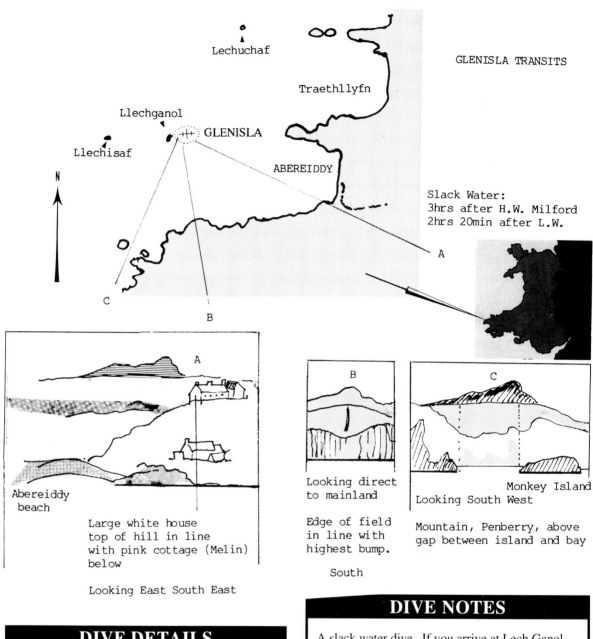

Lechuchaf

Traethllyfn

GLENISLA TRANSITS

Llechganol

GLENISLA

Llechisaf

ABEREIDDY

N

Slack Water:
3hrs after H.W. Milford
2hrs 20min after L.W.

A

C

B

A

Abereiddy
beach

Large white house
top of hill in line
with pink cottage (Melin)
below

Looking East South East

B

Looking direct
to mainland

Edge of field
in line with
highest bump.

South

C

Monkey Island

Looking South West

Mountain, Penberry, above
gap between island and bay

DIVE DETAILS

Location: 51° 56'09" N 05° 13'54" W
About 30 metres East of Lechganol
Depth: 15m to 20m
Seabed: rock and gravel
Currents: strong, up to 5 knots
Underwater Visibiliy: good
Launch Site: Porthgain or Abereiddy

DIVE NOTES

A slack water dive. If you arrive at Lech Ganol
(sometimes known as the Middle Sledge) at low
water there is more chance of locating it, it is then
a simple matter of dropping anchor about 30
metres east of the rock. The wreck is well broken
up and spread out. The 21 metre long prop shaft
lies in the centre of the wreck site at 16 metres
depth. Beware of returning to Abereiddy beach if
the swell has increased. Many dive boats have
capsized in the Abereiddy surf!

GOVERNOR FENNER

Type: Full Rigged Sailing Ship
Port of Registry: New York
Tonnage: 360 tons
Built: 1827, Rhode Island
Draught: 17 feet
Date of Sinking: February 20th 1841
Location: 15 miles west of Holyhead, Anglesey, Gwynedd

The American sailing ship GOVERNOR FENNER set sail from the quayside at Liverpool at 2pm on a Friday in February 1841. She was destined for New York, her home port, with a cargo of 400 tons of iron and 107 passengers. For many of the passengers it was the start of a new life for they were emigrating to the New World.

Captain Andrews was in command and had an American crew of 18 men all told. The ship made good progress until she had rounded the Anglesey coast. It was about 2am when they found themselves 15 miles west of Holyhead, in calm weather but a foggy dark night when the Captain was alerted to the lights of another vessel seen ahead on the weather-bow. The vessel was the paddle steamer NOTTINGHAM inward bound with passengers and livestock from Dublin. The helmsman of the steamer failed to distinguish the lights of the GOVERNOR FENNER and maintained his helm starboard at the same time as Captain Andrews was putting his helm over to avoid a collision. There was an almighty shudder as the bows and bowsprit of the GOVERNOR FENNER smashed into the starboard paddle box of the steamer. So violent was the impact that the steamer's funnel and wheelhouse was knocked over and her starboard engine and paddle-wheel were

The unidentified figurehead in the Gwynedd Maritime Museum may possibly have come from the GOVERNOR FENNER lost in Caernarfon Bay in 1841

shattered. The effect on the sailing ship was even more disastrous, her bows were stove in and within one minute of the impact she had sunk beneath the waves. Only Captain Andrews and the First Officer, Mr Carter, managed to survive, jumping onto the steamer as their own ship sank beneath them.

The horror of the moment is described in the words of Captain Carter, extracted from the Welshman dated 26th February 1841;
'I repaired (went) forward, and found the ship going down, head first. I instantly ordered the men on deck to save their lives but they still kept going abaft. I remained on the fo'castle until the ship was at the water's edge, and just saved my life by catching at a rope from the steamer. My Mate jumped from the foreyard on board the steamer and saved his life by so doing. All the passengers were in their berths and asleep at the moment they were thus hurried to eternity.'

The steamer NOTTINGHAM, besides passengers was carrying over 100 cattle and sheep, and many of the animals were killed at the time of the collision. In order to empty the steamer and clear her of all unnecessary cargo both the dead and the live animals were thrown overboard. The steamer managed to get into dock without further mishap.

HELVETIA

Type: Sailing Vessel, Barque Rigged
Port of Registry: Horten, Norway
Built: 1858, Bremerhaven
Length: 135 feet
Breadth: 28 feet
Date of Sinking: November 1st 1887
Location: Rhossili Beach, Gower, Glamorgan

In a tremendous storm that caused three supporting rods in the middle of the Clifton Suspension Bridge to snap, Captain Stevensen had a great dilemma. He was in charge of the barque HELVETIA outside Swansea flying signal flags for a pilot after completing an Atlantic crossing. He was attempting to get into Swansea, the destination for the 500 tons of timber cargo from New Brunswick. Although his signal flags were seen, the weather was too rough for the pilot cutter to leave the shelter of Swansea Bay.

During the Monday night flare up lights were burnt in the hope of getting a pilot, but failing to get one, and with a south easterly increasing he was forced to stand down Channel. At 8am the HELVETIA was near the Helwick Buoy with the wind blowing a strong gale and backing to the south west.

The barque was driven over the Helwick shoal where the seas and the pounding caused her to lose some of her deck load. Captain Stevensen managed to sail the battered ship around Worms Head into what would have been sheltered water had the wind stayed south easterly. In a smother of broken water the barque rounded the Head and let go her anchors on the north side of Worms Head. Luck was not with Captain Stevensen, the wind backed towards the west and the HELVETIA was too close to the rocks and struck them whilst at anchor.

The Coastguard and the Rocket Brigade stationed at Rhossili got their equipment across the sand onto Worms Head. There they fixed up a rocket line and brought one man ashore. The rest of the crew did not wish to leave but as the day progressed and the tide rose it became obvious to all that the vessel was not going to be saved. The remaining crewmen subsequently came ashore in the ship's rowing boats. At 5.30pm the HELVETIA parted from her anchors and drove ashore on the sands.

Planks of Canadian deal washed out of her hull and there was timber everywhere. In the weeks that followed all the cargo was salvaged, stacked above high water mark and later auctioned, much of it going to the original consignees, but at a greatly reduced price.

The hull timbers of the HELVETIA are still to be seen sticking out of the sand at the southern end of Rhossili Beach, a reminder of the hazards of the Bristol Channel for a large sailing vessel a century ago, however, this time it was without any loss of life.

The gaunt ribs of the HELVETIA still rise out of the sands on Rhossili beach over 100 years after she was wrecked. Worms Head is to be seen in the background
Photo: Tom Bennett

HMS BARKING

Type: Boom Defence Vessel
Place of Registry: Royal Navy
Tonnage: 730 tons displacement
Length: 173 feet
Breadth: 32 feet
Engines: Triple expansion, 850 hp
Date of Sinking: March 14th 1964
Location: Mill Bay, Milford Haven, Pembrokeshire, Dyfed

It is sometimes said that ships prefer to sink gracefully at sea rather than suffer the humiliation of the breakers yard. Certainly many ships have broken from their tow when on their final journey to the scrap yard, one such casualty was the Bibby Liner HEREFORDSHIRE wrecked on Cardigan Island in 1934 (see Volume 1), HMS BARKING thirty years later, was another.

HMS BARKING, was a Bar Class Boom Defence Vessel, one of 62 ships, built in the late 1930's and 1940's. All this class had names prefixed by the three letters BAR, but by 1965 only 19 were still in service. With powerful lifting capacities varying between 27 and 70 tons, these vessels had many uses including cable laying, degaussing and salvage. They had a compliment of 32, and with a total of 214 tons of coal fuel, had a range of 3,000 miles. In 1964, like others of her class, HMS BARKING was being 'deleted for disposal from the Naval list'.

She was being towed on her final trip to the 'Giant's Graveyard' of Thomas Ward at Briton Ferry when she broke from the tow in heavy seas. It happened in rough weather in March 1964 and men on the towing vessel were unable to get another line aboard her. The force 6 south easterly wind took the Admiralty vessel into Mill Bay, a rocky cove about half a mile from St Ann's Head at the entrance to Milford Haven. Fortunately there was no-one on board at the time but unfortunately for the salvors she came ashore at 9.15am, at the top of a high tide, and became badly holed on large boulders when she hit the beach. Efforts to refloat her were unsuccessful and she was abandoned for ten years, slowly breaking up where she lay on the beach. In 1974 a salvage firm removed most of the rusty hulk but to the consternation of local people left jagged pieces lying all over the beach. To this day if you walk down to Mill Bay you will see the odd piece of scrap steel lying amongst the boulders, the last remnants of this vessel. HMS BARKING may have had ideas of her own when breaking away from her tow in 1964, but her ultimate end was an ignominious one after all.

The cover picture of this book shows HMS BARKING in Mill Bay in 1964 soon after she came ashore.

HMS BARKING breaking up on the rocks near St. Ann's Head, in 1964, after breaking loose whilst being towed to the scrapyard.
Photo: Jim Silk

HINDLEA II

Type: Coasting Cargo Ship
Port of Registry: Cardiff
Official Number: 167106
Previous Names: FENNEL, SUFFOLKBROOK, EMPIRE ISLE
Tonnage: 402 tons gross
Built: 1941, Hessle
Length: 143 feet
Breadth: 26 feet
Date of Sinking: October 27th 1959
Location: Moelfre Point, Anglesey, Gwynedd

The HINDLEA was on passage from Weston Point, near Runcorn, Cheshire to Newport, Gwent, when she was caught in a particularly violent storm. The empty cargo ship was at anchor sheltering in Dulas Bay from a south westerly gale when the wind unexpectedly veered north. A hurricane blew and the HINDLEA was in trouble. Her Captain tried in vain to drive into the weather but the ship's propeller thrashed madly in the swell more out of the water than in and she made no headway. Soon she was rolling violently on one anchor cable and then at 12.11pm Seaford Radio received a message that she required assistance. Within 45 minutes the Moelfre Lifeboat was alongside.

The Lifeboat happened to be a Reserve Lifeboat while the other was undergoing a refit. Despite never having been on this Lifeboat before, the Coxswain, Dick Evans, commanded it in excellent style.

The sea was a boiling cauldron with waves eight metres high hitting the disabled ship and riding back. The Lifeboat was taken on her beam ends, her mast underwater, but Coxswain Evans persevered with his task. He manouvered the Lifeboat up to the HINDLEA's port quarter and at each run a member of the crew jumped aboard. At one stage the Lifeboat was taken clean over the decks of the HINDLEA. It was a brilliant rescue and the RNLI awarded Coxswain Evans a Gold Medal, Mechanic Owen a Silver Medal and Bronze Medals to three of the crew.

Half an hour after the 8 men had been rescued the ship was hurled with tremendous force against Moelfre Point where she broke into two pieces.

The day before this event the local village had attended a centenary Remembrance Service for those lost in the sinking of the ROYAL CHARTER in 1859. The HINDLEA was lost at almost the same spot exactly one hundred years later.

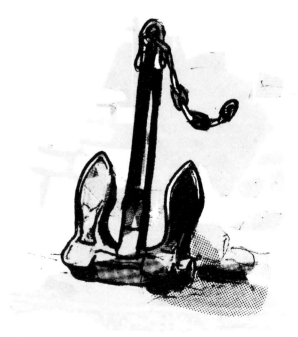

The HINDLEA anchor displayed at Moelfre. The anchor shank was bent during the shipwreck.

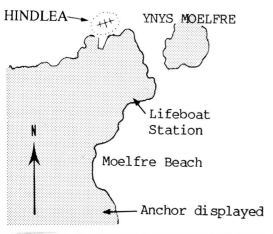

HINDLEA · YNYS MOELFRE

Lifeboat Station

Moelfre Beach

Anchor displayed

N

DIVE DETAILS

Location: 53° 21'39" N 04° 15'20" W
About 300 metres West of Ynys Moelfre.
Depth: 5m to 15m
Seabed: rock, sand & seaweed
Currents: negligible
Underwater Visibility: variable to poor
Launch Site: Moelfre

Only half an hour after a dramatic rescue of the crew by the Moelfre Lifeboat, the HINDLEA is smashed to pieces by the huge waves
Photo: Courtesy of Kinmel Arms, Moelfre

HORNBY

Type: Sailing Vessel, Brig Rigged
Port of Registry: Liverpool
Tonnage: 241 tons
Built: 1810, Chester
Date of Sinking: January 1st 1824
Location: Great Orme, Llandudno, Gwynedd

The Great Orme, has impressive cliffs rising abruptly out of the sea and its great height of over 200 metres makes it an imposing feature fully justifying its Viking name 'ormr', meaning serpent. In its shadow sailing vessels would shelter from the westerlies but in winds from the north it was a place to avoid. At its westernmost point is a cave known as Hornby Cave which is named after this vessel.

The brig HORNBY set out from her home port of Liverpool on December 27th 1823. Her Master was Captain Wade who was reported as being a disagreeable man; he had lived in Beaumaris where he was not popular. The general cargo was an expensive one, dry goods to the value of £60,000, which was outward bound to Rio de Janeiro. There was a crew of 13 with 2 passengers. When they reached Port Lynas, on the coast of Anglesey, they met with strong winds from the north west which prevented them from reaching the shelter of Holyhead. For two days they tried to make headway tacking back and forth between The Great Orme and Point Lynas. On the second night the Mate suggested to the Captain that they should go into Beaumaris for shelter. He got a curt rebuff from Captain Wade who replied 'I'd rather be at sea for ever than go there!'

The storm became even more severe and as midnight approached the conditions were so bad that the sailing vessel was driven against the rocks and cliffs of Great Orme Head where she sank. A contemporary account continues with the story; 'One of the crew happened at this moment to be out upon the bowsprit, in the act of either loosing or taking in the jib, and he was flung by the concussion upon a narrow shelf of rock, where he lay for some time stunned and confounded; but at length he succeeded in getting to the top of that frightful precipice, and crawled to a smithy at a little distance, where he was found at 5am by some workman employed there, in connection with a neighbouring copper-mine. He told his melancholy story, but was laughed at, for he could only say that he had climbed up the horrid steep which had wrecked the vessel; how, he knew not, and the thing appeared impossible to those acquainted with the place. At daylight, however, (for it was winter), portions of the wreck were discoverd near the spot, and the truth of man's story was shortly after made apparent. No other individual of the HORNBY'S crew, or thing belonging to her, was saved.'

The sole survivor's name was John Williams who gave up life on the sea and took up work in a foundry in Liverpool. In later life he lived off money from tourists who were intrigued to hear the true story of a real shipwrecked sailor.

HUDIKSVALL

Type: Sailing Ship, Barque Rigged
Port of Registry: Hudiksvall, Sweden
Tonnage: 1,363 tons net
Built: 1867, Honfleur, France
Length: 212 feet
Breadth: 33 feet
Date of Sinking: November 20th 1890
Location: Carmel Head, Anglesey, Gwynedd

In 1890 the RNLI established a second Lifeboat at Holyhead. It was in direct response to the increasing work load of the overstretched rescue services surrounding the Harbour. The first rescue for the newly established lifeboat was bold, daring and successful.

At 6pm on a stormy November evening distress signals were seen between the breakwater and the Skerries. In response, guns were fired by Mr Thomas at the Coastguard Station to muster the Lifeboat crew. The new Lifeboat JOSEPH WHITWORTH was launched within seven minutes with veteran Coxswain Edward Jones at the helm.

The ship in trouble was the Swedish barque HUDIKSVALL; commencing a voyage across the Atlantic from Liverpool to New York in ballast, she was forced into Holyhead to shelter from strong west south west winds. Her anchors failed to hold and the sailing vessel was driven northwards from her anchorage towards the rocks of Carmel Head.

By the time the Lifeboat reached her she was on her beam-ends with two masts gone and breaking up fast. The barque's crew had to struggle against the waves as the sea surged across the decks. The men desperately hung on, searching for a position on the uppermost part of the wreck from where they could be rescued. There was a small gap between the wreck and the rocks but the Lifeboat Coxswain bravely steered his boat between them, getting close enough to pass ropes to the men who had lashed themselves to the upper rails. A rope was fixed up and the men were able to slide down into the Lifeboat. Eventually all 16 men, one by one, were hauled to the safety of the Lifeboat, which subsequently landed them ashore at Holyhead at 9pm.

How to locate the HUDIKSVALL

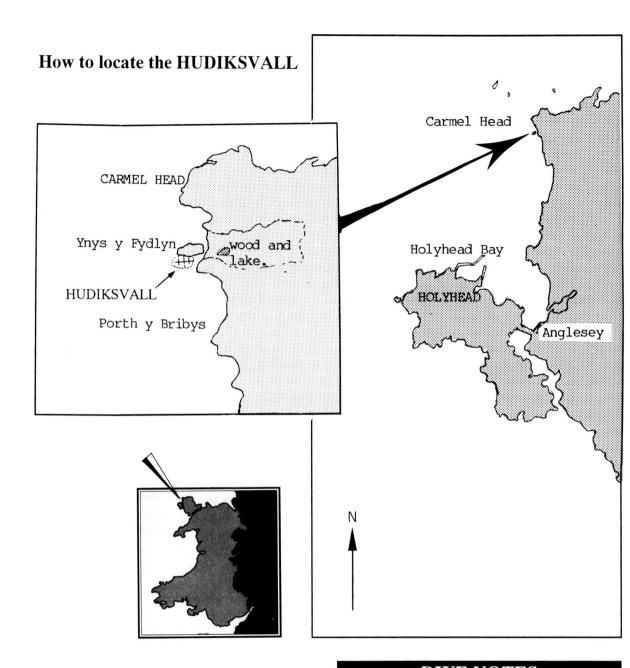

DIVE DETAILS

Location: 53° 23'40" N 04° 34'18" W
Depth: 12m to 21m
Seabed: rock
Currents: slight or none
Underwater Visibility: fair
Launch Site: Holyhead or Cemaes Bay

DIVE NOTES

A good novice dive site. Find the south west corner of Ynys y Fydlyn, the island outside the wooded area half a mile south of Carmel Head. Anchor in 6 metres, descend down rocks to wreck site scattered over a large area, depth 21 metres. Uncomfortable site in windy weather, takes about 20 minutes to reach by inflatable from Holyhead or Cemaes Bay.

KYLE PRINCE

Type: Steamer, Coaster
Port of Registry: Liverpool
Official Number: 128485
Previous Names: ITA, ROSALEEN
Tonnage: 409 tons
Built: 1908, Dublin
Length: 155 feet
Breadth: 24 feet
Engines: Compound 2 cylinder, 87 rhp
Date of Sinking: October 8th 1938
Location: Aberffraw, Anglesey, Gwynedd

With a cement cargo from the South Wales port of Barry, the coaster KYLE PRINCE experienced severe October westerlies on her last luckless voyage to her home port of Liverpool. On the way she was forced to shelter for a few days at Milford Haven. When she eventually reached Bardsey she met with big seas and high winds which made progress difficult.

Just when the going was getting tough a circulatory pipe which led to the engine room broke. While the engineers worked on the repair the stokehold began to flood. The engineers and firemen frantically bucketted the water away but heavy seas entered the engine room and the water level soon extinguished the furnaces. While his men made a human chain to the deck

Disabled in heavy seas the steamer KYLE PRINCE was driven onto the Anglesey coast, the Holyhead Lifeboat saved the crew.
Illustration: Brian Entwistle.

frantically passing out buckets of scalding water, Captain Henry Fisher put out distress signals announcing that the KYLE PRINCE required assistance and that his ship was without power. For seven hours it seemed as though his radio call for help had fallen on deaf ears and his hopes of a rescue faded. As each hour went by his ship settled deeper into the water and the gale force winds were taking them towards the Anglesey coast. Not only were his thoughts on the safety of his crew and his ship but his own 17 year old son, Donald, was one of the crew on that frightful voyage. When nearing the coast, both anchors were dropped and distress rockets were fired but no acknowledgment of the signals were seen by the nine men on board.

Unknown to the steamer's crew the Holyhead Lifeboat CITY OF BRADFORD (1) was already on her way. When she met up with the KYLE PRINCE they were in mountainous seas and it required great skill on the part of Coxswain, Richard Jones, to get the Lifeboat near enough to perform a rescue. With four runs alongside the bucking steamer all nine men managed to jump from the rails into the safety of the Lifeboat.

The sea showed no mercy on the abandoned KYLE PRINCE, when her anchor cables snapped she was driven onto the cliffs at Caethle, near Aberffraw, where she became lodged between rocks and started to break up. Although her decks remained above water for some days, long enough for some loads of timber to be salvaged, her hull was a total loss and soon the seas smashed her into the rocks.

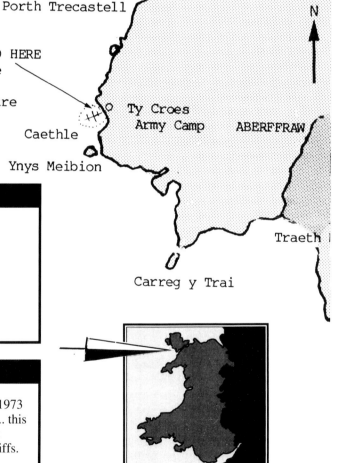

KYLE PRINCE WRECKED HERE
Look for the large white spherical structure on the cliff, like a 10 metre diameter Golf Ball.

DIVE DETAILS

Location: 53° 11'26" N 04° 30'18" W
Depth: 7m to 11m
Seabed: rock, sand & boulders
Currents: negligible on the wreck
Underwater visibility: generally good
Launch Site: Trearddur Bay or Rhosneigr at
High Water.

DIVE NOTES

The wreck has been extensively salvaged in 1973 but ribs are prominent out of the concretion ... this is proper concrete from the solidified cement cargo ! The stern of the wreck lies into the cliffs. Very exposed site to westerlies and uncomfortable in swells.

LEYSIAN

Type: Cargo Steamship
Port of Registry: Liverpool
Previous Name: SAREK
Tonnage: 4,703 tons
Built: 1906
Length: 400 feet
Breadth: 52 feet
Engines: Triple expansion, 477 nhp
Date of Sinking: February 20th 1917
Location: Abercastle, Pembrokeshire, Dyfed

One of the largest steamers to hit directly into the cliffs of North Pembrokeshire was the LEYSIAN in 1917. She had discharged horses and mules at Belfast and was heading south for Barry Roads when an error, in the fog, was to cause her downfall. Strumble Head foghorn was blasting out but those on board mistook it for one near St David's. About forty minutes later there was an almighty shudder in the coastal village of Abercastle, plates fell off the dressers and everyone thought there was an earthquake. The earth did shake but it was the force of the 4,700 ton LEYSIAN crashing into the rocks half a mile away.

The LEYSIAN, originally named SAREK, had been taken over from German ownership by F.Leyland and Company early in World War 1; when she hit the rocky headland the force pierced a large hole in her bows. An Admiralty patrol vessel and the Fishguard Lifeboat went to the rescue although none of the 130 men aboard were in any immediate danger. The LEYSIAN had grounded in water that was only 3 metres deeper than her draught of 8 metres, she could not sink more than a few feet. The Lifeboat made three trips, taking 80 cattlemen and crew to Fishguard and others were taken overland by bus. An attempt was made to refloat her, but without success and the wreck remained upright and intact for seven months until a fierce October gale broke her up.

Her remains now lie scattered on the seabed, under the rocks where she grounded, and provide interesting homes for lobsters and wrasse. The wreck is also a suitable dive site for divers of all abilities.and it is a convenient location to dive in rough weather from the south or west as the large cliffs provide shelter from winds from these directions. However ground swells and big tides tend to make for poor underwater visibility and there can be a lot of fine sediment all over the wreck site.

How to locate the LEYSIAN.

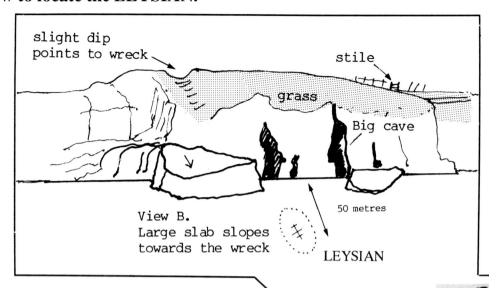

slight dip points to wreck

stile

grass

Big cave

View B.
Large slab slopes towards the wreck

LEYSIAN

50 metres

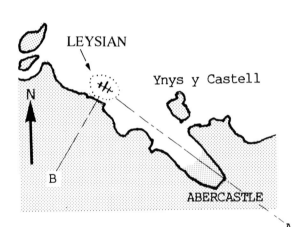

LEYSIAN

Ynys y Castell

N

B

ABERCASTLE

A

The wreck lies about halfway between Abercastle beach and the island on the left hand headland.

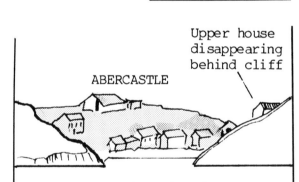

Upper house disappearing behind cliff

ABERCASTLE

View A. Back to beach most of houses can be seen.

DIVE DETAILS

Location: 51° 57'36" N 05° 07'52" W
Depth: 10m to 13m
Seabed: silt and rock
Currents: slight
Underwater visibility: often poor
Launch Site: Abercastle or Porthgain

DIVE NOTES

A convenient wreck site to dive when rough weather prevents going further afield. Can be dived at all states of the tide and by all abilities. Spring tides impair underwater visibility.

LINNET

Type: Sailing Vessel, Sloop Rigged
Port of Registry: Cardigan
Tonnage: 40 tons
Built: 1820, Ceibach, near New Quay
Date of Sinking: November 7th 1890
Location: Lavan Sands, Gwynedd

Returning to her home port of Aberaeron with a general cargo from Liverpool the smack LINNET became caught in a ferocious gale which resulted in her loss and the loss of one of those on board. The gale hit her when she was rounding the Anglesey coast and driven back by the wind and heavy seas Captain Abraham Thomas decided to anchor near Red Wharfe Bay. There were just three on board, Captain Thomas, the mate and a twelve year old boy, all from Aberaeron. The three were soaked to the skin and thoroughly exhausted and when the anchor broke loose they were in no condition to respond. The vessel drifted passed Puffin Island and on to Lavan Sands about 2 miles from Beaumaris.

They stranded on the sands in the midst of a severe storm. In Holyhead the wind was causing 'chimney pots and slates to be flying about in all directions'. But the people on dry land were the lucky ones, those at sea were fighting for their lives and the three on board the LINNET were no exception.

The local newspaper takes up the story.
'The storm raged with great fury about 1am, the sea washing over the deck and threatening to sweep all away. They then lashed the boy to the rigging. In about two hours, in response to his heart rending cries, and the storm somewhat abating, he was released, and was nursed by the mate for one hour. He was once more lashed to the rigging as being the only chance for life and his cries during the night of suffering were most

A sloop deliberately run ashore onto a sandy beach in a gale. The LINNET would have looked like this.
Photo: Tom Bennett Collection

pitiful, and about 6am they entirely ceased - death coming at last to release him.'

A similar fate would undoubtedly have befallen Captain Thomas and the Mate if help had not arrived. Two local men, at daylight, had seen a wreck lying high and dry and hurried out over sand to help. They had in fact seen another wreck 600 metres away, the crew of which were alive but too weak to help. This crew offered their small boat to the rescuers to get over the channels to reach the LINNET which they managed to do in time to save Captain Thomas and the Mate, before they too died of hypothermia.

LUMINENCE

Type: General Cargo Vessel
Port of Registry: London
Tonnage: 558 tons
Built: 1954, Wallsend-on-Tyne
Length: 190 feet
Breadth: 28 feet
Date of Sinking: March 1st 1967
Location: Hats and Barrels, Pembrokeshire, Dyfed

The British motor general cargo vessel LUMINENCE left the East Yelland Power Station in North Devon at 8am on St Davids Day 1967. The vessel, owned by the London and Rochester Trading Company, was in ballast and was going north to Ayr in Scotland.

The weather was rough, with 40 mph winds and midway through the afternoon she passed the Pembrokeshire coast, a few miles east of the Smalls Lighthouse when she hit the submerged rock known as the Hats.

The LUMINENCE hit the rock at about 3.40pm and immediately listed heavily to starboard. Fearing she was going to sink quickly the eight man crew radioed a Mayday for help, abandoned their vessel and got aboard the ship's liferaft. The sea was boisterous with 15 foot waves tossing the inflatable liferaft like a cork as it drifted away from the sinking vessel. St David's Lifeboat was launched but help came from the Royal Naval Air Station at Brawdy who immediately sent out a helicopter. The helicopter pilot, Lieutenant Derek Scott, spotted the liferaft and hovered over the spot while the men, one by one, were winched to safety. The survivors were transferred to the 10,110 ton cargo ship PATROCLUS which was nearby and had been diverted for the rescue. The PATROCLUS crew had to lower one of her masts in order to allow the helicopter sufficient room to winch the men down. It was a brilliant and successful rescue, within 90 minutes of the LUMINENCE striking the rock, the crew were safely aboard another vessel. As one of the crew was being lowered onto the PATROCLUS, the men could see the LUMINENCE keel over and sink beneath the waves.

The official time of sinking and location given for the LUMINENCE is 17.05 hrs on March 1st at Lat 51° 41'20" N. Long 05° 32'20" W.

The LUMINENCE hit the Hats, off the Pembrokeshire coast, in March 1967. Seen here with a heavy starboard list minutes after the crew abandoned, the coaster sank half an hour later.

Photo: Royal Naval Air Station. Brawdy.

MARY

Type: Royal Yacht
Place of Registry: Royal Navy
Tonnage: 100 tons
Built: prior to 1660, Holland
Length: 52 feet
Breadth: 19 feet
Draught: 8 feet
Date of Sinking: March 25 1675
Location: Skerries, off Anglesey, Gwynedd

In 1660, Charles II was so taken with the idea of having a yacht that it prompted the Burgomaster of Amsterdam to present him with one. Named MARY, it was a magnificent vessel, extremely fast with a splendid unicorn adorning her bows. She was fitted out in a most luxurious manner by the finest Dutch craftsmen with a four berth state cabin decorated with gold leaf and upholstered with fifty metres of leather, beautifully tooled and gilded. MARY was described by Samuel Pepys as 'one of the finest things I ever saw for neatness and room in a small vessel'. In 1661 she was transferred to the Royal Navy to be used as transport for nobility and government officials.

It was a foggy night in March 1675 when the MARY, taking passengers from Dublin to Chester, ran onto a rock on the Out Skerries. It was in the middle of the night and most were below decks asleep when they hit the rock. The vessel partially sank and listed heavily causing the tall mast to make a bridge onto one of the rocks. The Master, Captain Burlow, tried to help one of the passengers, the Earl of Meath, across the mast to safety but they were both lost in the attempt, and a further 33 people also lost their lives. 15 passengers and 24 sailors got onto the island but then had to endure further distress as they were not rescued for two days. During that time they managed to light a fire using some gunpowder from a flask, a steel and bits of timber from the wrecked ship. Rescue eventually came in the form of an Irish vessel that was sailing from Beaumaris and happened to see them. They were returned to Beaumaris.

The wreck site today is a protected one under the Protection of Wrecks Act and diving is only allowed with special permission. To help protect the site, the exact location is not included here. In Liverpool Maritime Museum there is a display of artefacts recovered by divers from the MARY site, it includes silver forks, pewter plates, coins, lockets, rings, and a pewter chamber pot!

MISSOURI

Type: Steamer, 4 Masted Screw Barque
Official Number: 84104
Tonnage: 5,146 tons gross
Built: 1881, Glasgow
Length: 426 feet
Breadth: 44 feet
Engines: Compound Steam, 600 hp
Date of Sinking: March 1st 1886
Location: Porth Dafarch, Anglesey, Gwynedd

Built by the C.Connel Shipbuilding Company in 1881, the MISSOURI was a magnificent iron ship for her day. Barque rigged with four masts she had a single funnel stack and a large 600 horsepower engine. She was sturdily built, with no less than seven bulkheads, and intended to withstand Atlantic gales. Although her lifespan was a short one of only five years, she did prove to be a strong ship just as her owners, G.Warren & Co., had intended. Her downfall, however, as with so many other fine ships, was human error.

The Warren Line steamer MISSOURI was returning from Boston, USA with a mixed cargo

Returning from America, the White Diamond steamer MISSOURI was driven off course by a dense fog and snowstorm. She landed ashore on the Anglesey coast at Porth Dafarch, where her remains still lie.

Photo: Henry Parry Collection, Gwynedd Archives Service

of live cattle, hides, palm oil and bales of cotton. With the open expanse of the Atlantic behind him, Captain Kerr was now sailing north up St George's Channel with only one day's sailing before seeing the lights of the Mersey.

The Captain was not to know that weather conditions were to deteriorate to the worst for twenty years. A south westerly gale was blowing which took them quickly across Cardigan Bay but then a dense fog and a driving snowstorm caught them unawares and navigation turned into a nightmare. A course was set to clear the coast by two miles, but due allowance for tide and leeway was not made. With visibility reduced to only a few metres the ship struck the Anglesey coast near Porth Dafarch, a position three miles east of the intended course.

Captain Kerr made attempts to extract the MISSOURI from the rocks using the single screw propeller but this had the effect of bringing the stern around to meet the shore.

In an attempt to lighten the ship some of the cattle were released and driven over the side into the water. There were three hundred and ninety five head of cattle and about a quarter of them were thrown overboard. This White Diamond steamer had hit the rocks only a few miles, overland, from Holyhead, and the cliff rescue team and tugs were soon on the scene to help.

A breeches buoy was rigged up and the ship's Doctor, 18 cattlemen and 3 stowaways were safely hauled ashore. Captain Kerr and the crew stayed on board while two tugs tried all day to tow the stricken ship off the rocks. They failed, and at midnight the hull suddenly moved and started to list to starboard. Quickly the crew abandoned the ship as she settled onto her beam. All the men managed to escape in boats but the majority of the cattle still on board were drowned, only fifty of them were saved.

To extract the bales of cotton and other cargo a large hole was blasted through the iron plated hull using explosives. After a month of salvage work some of the cargo was recovered. The MISSOURI finally broke apart and her iron parts now litter the seabed providing a popular shallow underwater attraction for experienced and novice divers alike.

The strength of the MISSOURI's iron hull caused something of a problem for those responsible for the salvage of the valuable cargo. As the hull had fallen over on her starboard side (as the accompanying photograph shows), there was a valuable cargo of hides and cotton trapped between decks still to be recovered.

It was decided to make an access hole through the hull to salvage the cargo and the thickness and strength of the plates made it a difficult task. Various holes were cut using gun cotton, put in place by Royal Naval gunners. After much effort a sufficient sized hole was made using 80 lbs of commercial dynamite. The salvage work could now commence. The easy access into the hull was an attraction to many of the local people under cover of darkness. Due to the diligence of the Senior Coastguard Officer, who fired shots from his revolver in making the arrests, a number of men were tried for theft at the local Court. One man, William Ellis, was convicted of stealing two hides and a bag full of suet. Others were convicted of stealing flour, and had fines ranging from 10/- to £1.

After a month of salvage work the wreck was abandoned to the sea, breaking up in her exposed position to the prevailing gales.

This wreck has probably been visited by more divers than any other in North Wales, yet it still provides a popular dive site, being convenient to a launching beach and a good novice dive site.

How to locate the MISSOURI

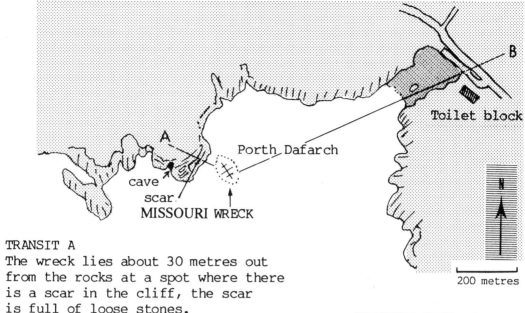

TRANSIT A
The wreck lies about 30 metres out
from the rocks at a spot where there
is a scar in the cliff, the scar
is full of loose stones.

MISSOURI WRECK SITE

TRANSIT B
When looking North East back to the beach,
a white house is just visible on the right.
Toilet block is hidden by a pointed rock
on the left hand side.

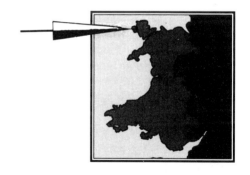

DIVE DETAILS

Location: 53° 17'01" N 04° 39'18" W
         On North side of Porth Dafarch.
Depth: 6m to 13m
Seabed: rock & sand
Currents: negligible
Underwater Visibility: fair to good
Launch Site: Porth Dafarch or Trearddur

DIVE NOTES

A popular dive site and one for novices, but the
sandy seabed surrounding the spread out is
uninteresting. The outline of the boilers can still
be seen and a large part of the bow section. The
remainder is iron plates and parts of the masts.

MYSTIC TIE

Type: Sailing Ship, Brigantine Rigged
Port of Registry: Ardrossan
Official Number: 69198
Tonnage: 345 tons gross
Built: 1874
Length: 115 feet
Breadth: 30 feet
Date of Sinking: November 11th 1877
Location: Ramsey Island, St David's, Pembrokeshire, Dyfed

Laden with a cargo of palm oil from West Africa the brigantine MYSTIC TIE had gone to Queenstown, near Cork for orders before setting sail once more for Le Havre. While she was in the western approaches she met a severe storm. So atrocious was the weather that all her sails were blown to ribbons and she was completely at the mercy of the sea and the wind.

The brigantine drifted onto the rocks at the southern end of Ramsey Sound at 4pm on a Sunday afternoon. The seas were rough and her hull was pounded by the waves, with surf washing over her decks.

The Captain and one man jumped overboard and managed to reach the safety of the island but another African seaman who tried to follow was drowned. The remaining 7 crewmen decided to stay with the wreck and clung on as best they could hoping that the seas would calm down. The Lifeboat Station at St Justinian could see the distress signals from the island but because the sea was too ferocious they decided not to launch.

At 6.30pm the MYSTIC TIE finally broke apart and the mate and 6 crew managed to scramble onto a rocky outcrop, where they spent a miserable night.

In the morning the St David's Lifeboat AUGUSTA went out to the rescue. Her Coxswain David Hicks decided to take extra crewmen as the weather was so bad. It was the right decision as it took the ten-oared Lifeboat four hours to get to the men that were on a rock less than two miles away. When they eventually got near to the wreck the waves were too high for them to carry out a rescue. Each time they tried to get near to the rock they were forced to back off. After a further two hours of straining at the oars they made a final attempt. Using a throwing line loaded into a hollow cane the Lifeboat Bowman threw a life-line over to the survivors.

Lines were rigged up and 6 men were hauled through the surf into the Lifeboat. As the seventh man was being rescued the lifelines got trapped around his foot. Captain Hicks acted

St David's Lifeboat plaque showing entry of MYSTIC TIE

swiftly and decisively, taking the Lifeboat into the surf while the bowman cut the lines tangled around the man's foot. They got him aboard and returned to the mainland.

This was just one of many successful rescues undertaken by Coxswain Hicks in the AUGUSTA which was on service at St David's from 1869 to 1885. David Hicks was Coxswain for twenty three years and on retirement he retained his memories with the Lifeboat. When the AUGUSTA was due to be replaced he bought her for use as a chicken shed in his garden!

David Hicks, St David's Lifeboat Coxwain for 23 years.
Photo: R.N.L.I.

A ten-oared pulling lifeboat. The AUGUSTA lifeboat at St Davids (1869 - 1885) was of this type.
Illustration: R.N.L.I.

NETHER HOLME

Type: Steel Screw Steamer
Port of Registry: Maryport
Official Number: 89478
Tonnage: 1,969 tons register
Built: 1888, Sunderland
Length: 277 feet
Breadth: 37 feet
Date of Sinking: November 3rd 1907
Location: Linney Head, Pembrokeshire, Dyfed

The NETHER HOLME was owned by the Cardiff shipowners of M.Thomas and Son Shipping Company. On a quiet autumn day in 1907, Captain V. Lauder was in command as she steamed south from Maryport, her port of registry, to Swansea. A sea mist prevailed so he took the precaution of making regular depth soundings. On approaching St Govan's Head he saw the light and heard the fog signals but assumed them to be those of Lundy as he did not know that the St Govan's Light had been established. Hastily and erroneously he altered course and, thinking he was passing Lundy, ran the NETHER HOLME directly onto the platform of rocks at Penyholt, near Linney Head.

Fortunately, all the crew were able to climb off the steamer at low tide and were then able to scale the cliffs above by means of a rope that had been left there by salvors working on the steamer SHAMROCK the year before. Although the NETHER HOLME lay exposed to all winds from south east to west, the weather was settled and the Salvage Association Surveyor decided that it was worth taking a chance to save her. With wet weather, a smooth sea and an easterly wind the salvors started work on November 8th. By the following night they had patched up the hull plates beneath the engine room and had floated her off and got her safely beached at Milford Haven.

The 'no cure, no pay' contract had worked, and she was one of the few steamers to be refloated from this part of the coast. Although the salvage was successful the ship had suffered on the rocks and the decision was taken to scrap her in March 1908.

The NETHER HOLME on the rocks at Penyholt
Photo: Pembrokeshire County Museums

NIMROD

Type: Paddle Steamer, 3 Masted Schooner Rig
Port of Registry: Cork, Ireland
Tonnage: 583 tons gross
Built: 1843, Liverpool
Length: 177 feet
Breadth: 25 feet
Engines: 300 nhp
Date of Sinking: February 27th 1860
Location: St David's Head, Pembrokeshire, Dyfed

Contemporary drawing of the NIMROD in 1843

It was 10pm on the night of February 27th 1860 when Captain Pearn in command of the CITY OF PARIS, a Cork to Milford ferry, sighted the paddle steamer NIMROD about 15 miles off the Smalls Lighthouse. He could see the NIMROD had her sails set and that her engines had stopped. He investigated, hailed her and enquired of Captain Lyall of the NIMROD if he could be of assistance. The reply came, 'What will you tow us into Milford for?' Captain Pearn said '£1,000', to which Captain Lyall offered £100. 'It is out of the question' replied Captain Pearn 'but I'll tow you to Milford and leave the remuneration to be settled by the owners'. This was not accepted by Captain Lyall who then requested that Captain Pearn report the

NIMROD's engine failure on his arrival at Waterford. Captain Lyall's decision to decline assistance was a decision he was to regret before the night was over.

The weather was moderate and Captain Lyall, a Scotsman who had been with the Cork Steamship Company for many years, was confident of sailing to Milford without assistance. The NIMROD had left Liverpool at 10am the previous morning with passengers and general cargo for Cork, when, in the middle of St George's Channel, and out of sight of land, the engine developed trouble and finally stopped. This was not the first time the 300 horse power engine had caused problems. Some four years before, on the same route, there had been a boiler explosion ripping the engine room apart and killing 6 people.

During the night the wind increased and bad weather loomed before them. The force of the wind, already a strong westerly, increased to a storm and the already crippled NIMROD could make no headway. Helpless, the disabled paddle steamer with 45 people on board was slowly driven towards the cliffs of St David's Head.

At 8am some residents of St David's hurried to the headland with the news that a shipwreck was imminent. By the time they arrived it was too late. What they saw was a scene of horror and chaos. The NIMROD had been pounded to bits on the rocks 100 feet beneath them. There was no way down the cliff and there was nothing any of them could do but watch the pitiful sight of the people drowning before them.

News got back to William Williams, acting Lloyd's agent and Coastguard, who immediately asked if the Manby rocket apparatus should be taken. The reply was that by the time it could get there the people would already be saved or dead. Mr Williams took a horse and galloped the few miles to the cliff top, what he then saw is best described in his own words. 'On my arrival there was not a vestige of the wreck to be seen. The vessel had already parted into three pieces, had gone down in deep water, and every soul had perished.' It was also reported that Captain Lyall

was last seen clutching at the stern rail with his head in his hands.

Among the passengers that drowned was a woman who happened to be on board because of a somewhat odd occurrence the previous week. Her husband was Captain Wigham, of the schooner WENSLEYDALE which was bound for Bremen with logwood when he became insane on the Atlantic crossing. The schooner put into Cobh, Ireland, where the ship's agents put him into lodgings. The owners contacted his wife in Newcastle and she travelled to Liverpool only just in time to catch the NIMROD as it was leaving the quay. The unfortunate woman never arrived in Ireland to nurse her poor husband. The cargo of general goods, which was irretrievable, was worth £7,000, the Company had insured it for £5,000. The NIMROD herself had undergone a thorough refit only 12 months previously and was worth £12,000. In August 1873, some 13 years after the event, divers were employed to recover machinery and valuable articles from the wreck, unfortunately we do not know how successful they were.

The Board of Trade Inquiry accepted the evidence given to them by those aboard the CITY OF PARIS. Captain Pearn said that had he for a moment envisaged such an awful calamity, no thought of money would have crossed his mind when considering a tow. Likewise the Court considered that Captain Lyall would not have declined the CITY OF PARIS's offer had he forseen the slightest danger to his ship, passengers or crew.

Square porthole from the stern of the NIMROD

Plate, oil lamp, bottle and brass barrel tap from the wreck site

How to locate the NIMROD

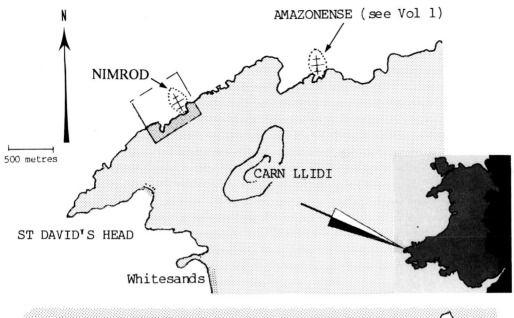

AMAZONENSE (see Vol 1)

N

500 metres

NIMROD

CARN LLIDI

ST DAVID'S HEAD

Whitesands

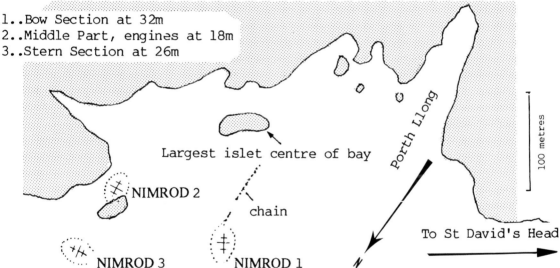

1..Bow Section at 32m
2..Middle Part, engines at 18m
3..Stern Section at 26m

Largest islet centre of bay

Porth Llong

100 metres

NIMROD 2

chain

NIMROD 3

NIMROD 1

To St David's Head

N

DIVE DETAILS

Location: 51° 54' 36" N 05° 17' 54" W
North East of St David's Head 0.8 nautical mile.
Depth: 18m to 32m
Seabed: rock, silt & gravel
Currents: strong on deep part
Underwater Visibility: good
Launch Site:
    from Porthgain   5.2 nautical miles
    from Whitesands   1.8 nautical miles
    from Porthclais   6 nautical miles

DIVE NOTES

The NIMROD 2 site can be dived at all states of the tide, but if you are diving the other two deeper sections you have to do so at slack which is difficult to judge.
To dive the deeper bow section (NIMROD 1) descend down the western edge of the rock island in the centre of the bay and go north. If you find the chain follow its direction to the wreck, it disappears in sand but keep going, the wreck is about 100 metres out from the rock.

NUEVO TORCUVATO

Type: Sailing Ship, Barque Rigged
Port of Registration: Valentia, Spain
Date of Sinking: December 7th 1856
Location: White Bank, Saundersfoot, Pembrokeshire, Dyfed

Some exceptional rescues were performed by the Tenby Lifeboatmen in the first Lifeboat to be stationed at Tenby. The Lifeboat, a twenty eight foot rowing boat carried a crew of 12, ten of whom provided the oar power. A strong south westerly gale was blowing on a Sunday night in December 1856. Anticipating trouble at sea, the Coxswain, Robert Parrott, took the Lifeboat out of the boathouse at Penniless Cove and had her waiting on the carriage at the top of the beach. At 8pm a vessel was reported to have run aground on a submerged sandbank to the east of Saundersfoot. It was an hour after low water and the Lifeboat was soon run down into the water and launched off the carriage. The Lifeboatmen were compelled to row around St Catherine's Island and then they had a flood tide and a heavy cross sea to battle with. With waves crashing constantly upon them it took the lifeboat crew about an hour to get seaward of St Catherine's Island.

Once out to sea they made for a position windward of the wreck which was a square rigged Spanish vessel named NUEVO TORCUVATO, which had run bows-on to the sandbank. The Lifeboatmen dropped anchor and backed their boat down on the wreck. What then happened is best described by the Lifeboat Coxswain, 'We should have made quick work now but, unfortunately, the mainsail boom and gaff were washed over the lee quarter, in backing clear of which, to avoid being stove, a sea struck us on the broadside, going over us, the force of which broke three of our lee oars, leaving us clear of the loose wreck. Here we found the benefit of our anchor, for the next sea would have thrown us on the strand but for the anchor bringing us up'. Having luckily escaped this danger they got out a hand grapnel and threw it over the wreck to enable the Lifeboat to be brought alongside. Despite the fact that seas were washing clean over the barque's stern all the 9 crew were taken off.

The Lifeboatmen then had the strenuous task of hauling their lifeboat out through the surf on the anchor before rowing out to windward and back to Tenby. It was a successful rescue and Coxswain Parrott had great praise for his men, the incident also gave him added confidence in his Lifeboat. He stated 'The boat behaved admirably; in fact, I am persuaded the crew would cheerfully face any sea in her when it is possible to row ahead'.

Each of the crew received £1 for their gallant services from the National Lifeboat Institution.

The NUEVO TORCUVATO broke up in the surf, to the east of Saundersfoot, within two hours of the men leaving her.

On December 7th 1856, anticipating trouble at sea, the Tenby Coxswain prepared the lifeboat on its carriage at the top of the beach
Etching: Tom Bennett Collection.

That evening in a southwesterly gale the Tenby crew carried out a strenuous rescue to save the crew of the NUEVO TORCUVATO
Illustration: R.N.L.I.

OCEAN

Type: Sailing Vessel, Smack Rigged
Port of Registry: Cardigan
Official Number: 9240
Tonnage: 33 tons
Built: 1827, Aberaeron
Length: 44 feet
Date of Sinking: October 2nd 1895
Location: Near Poppit Sands, Cardigan

The OCEAN was one of three Cardigan registered vessels bearing that name which traded during the middle of the last century. Built at Aberaeron, she survived the rigours of the sea for 68 years before being lost on the doorstep of her home port in 1895.

During her varied life there was an incident at Fishguard in November 1882 when her 2 crew had to be rescued by the Lifeboat. They were not alone however, the Fishguard Lifeboat took a total of 46 men off fifteen different vessels in one hectic day! It was thirteen years later when the OCEAN met her final resting place.

At Llangrannog the previous day the OCEAN had discharged a cargo of culm, an anthracite coal dust mixed with clay and burnt on the local house fires or used in the lime kilns, lime being needed to neutralize acidic soils. The unloading was a dirty, messy job but the hired men and the horses and carts were well accustomed to the work. The men knew that it was the last cargo of the season for the aged smack. Little did they realize it was to be her final trip to Llangrannog.

The vessel was owned by Mr Evan Jenkins of the Pentre Arms, who, like other innkeepers in the neighbourhood of Llangrannóg was both merchant and shipowner.

After discharging, the OCEAN, with just Captain Daniel Davies and the Mate on board, headed for the River Teifi where the vessel was to be laid-up for the winter months. They anchored about one mile outside the Cardigan bar, waiting for the morning tide. Just after midnight a dreadful gale blew up and by 2am it was howling from the north west. Trapped inside the bay with a heavy sea running they were forced to show distress signals.

Having showed the signals for half an hour with no response from the Coastguard station the 2 men decided to abandon the smack and take to their boat. They landed near to the Lifeboat station and soon afterwards the OCEAN parted her cables. She was blown ashore onto Black Rocks near Poppit Sands and smashed into splinters. The publican, Evan Jenkins, had lost his trading smack and it was uninsured.

OLINDA

Type: Liner Steamship, Barque Rigged
Port of Registry: Liverpool
Tonnage: 1,138 tons
Built: 1853
Date of Sinking: January 26th 1854
Location: Harry Furlough's Reef, Cemlyn, Anglesey, Gwynedd

One of the finest liners of her day was the OLINDA. She was built in 1853 for the princely sum of £35,000. It was a Pilot error, only nine months later, that caused her loss.

The OLINDA was steaming outward from her home port of Liverpool when rough winter weather prevented the Liverpool Pilot from disembarking at Point Lynas, his usual practice. The Pilot was very experienced, in fact he had twenty five years' experience, and, instead of taking a course seaward of the Skerries, he decided to take the tricky inner channel. It was a decision he was to regret for, at 8.45pm on a severe January evening in 1854, the OLINDA hit the rocks.

The North Wales Chronicle condenses the facts, 'Built for the conveyance of passengers and goods to Lisbon and the Brazils she was commanded by Captain Haram. She is universally pronounced to have been among the best appointed and furnished ships that ever left the British coasts. She sailed from Liverpool at

A pilot error caused the loss of the OLINDA in 1854. The Cemlyn Lifeboat seen astern of the wreck, saved the crew and passengers.
Illustration: Gwynedd Archives Service

noon on the January 26th and met with bad weather up to Point Lynas, when it moderated a little, though still continuing dark and squally. She was in the charge of an experienced Liverpool Pilot, who from some strange fatality, kept close to the Anglesey coast, instead of standing outside the Skerries. The consequence of such temerity was, that at 9pm, she took the ground on some rocks inside Harry's Furlong about 200 yards from high water mark. She immediately fired signal guns of distress, and showed blue lights which soon brought a Liverpool pilot schooner within a short distance of her and by 10pm the Cemlyn Lifeboat'. The OLINDA'S iron hull had hit the rocky reef with an abrupt thud. The passengers, who, moments before were preparing for their first night on a long voyage, were suddenly thrown into a state of shock and confusion. Panic subsided somewhat when the 66 people on board realized that the ship was not sinking and within an hour all the passengers had been taken off, into the ship's lifeboats and into the Cemlyn Lifeboat (a boat can be seen rowing away from the OLINDA in the accompanying picture). The

Captain, two Mates and the Pilot remained on board throughout the night and were able to wade ashore early next morning. With the falling tide the OLINDA'S hull pivoted round so that her bows pointed back to the east.

She was carrying a mixed cargo worth £50,000 to South America and most of the very valuable cargo was salvaged although some of it was damaged. The important mail was unloaded before it got damaged by the seawater and was returned to Holyhead. The entire loss of the ship and part of her cargo amounted to a little under £100,000.

The gash in her starboard side was too extensive to be repaired and the OLINDA, less than a year old, was left to the ravages of the waves.

The Pilot was blamed for her loss and it is ironic that under normal circumstances he would have disembarked from the steamer at Point Lynas but on this occasion bad weather had prevented him from doing so and he had remained in charge until the time of the stranding.

DIVE DETAILS

Location: 53° 24'55" N 04° 15'12" W
About 200 metres South West of Harry Furlough's Rock.
Depth: 6m to 18m
Seabed: rock & seaweed
Currents: strong, 4 knots
Underwater Visibility: variable
Launch Site:

from Cemaes Bay	2 nautical miles
from Bull Bay	5½ nautical miles
from Holyhead	8½ nautical miles

DIVE NOTES

High Water Slack is about 30 minutes after High Water Holyhead (or 10 minutes before H.W.Liverpool), then it runs West. Low Water Slack is about 5 minutes before High Water Holyhead, then tidal stream runs East. The Bangor schooner CHARLOTTE ANN was another victim on this reef in 1887.

How to find the OLINDA wreck site

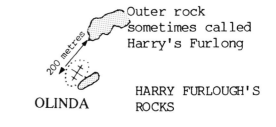

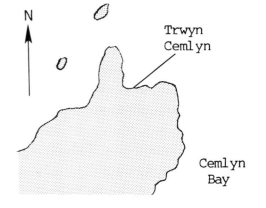

PRINCE CADWGAN

Type: Cargo Steamship
Port of Registry: Aberystwyth
Official Number: 48925
Tonnage: 111 tons gross, 75 tons net
Built: 1864, Glasgow
Length: 109 feet
Breadth: 19 feet
Engines: 2 cylinder Steam
Date of Sinking: September 30th 1876
Location: Carreg Frân, near Porthclais, Pembrokeshire, Dyfed

The arrival of the new PRINCE CADWGAN into Aberaeron in 1864 was a momentous occasion. It was the start of the steamer trade for the recently formed Aberayron Steam Navigation Company Ltd and an important stepping stone for the commercial economy of the port. All the four hundred £10 shares in the company had been taken up, mainly by Aberaeron businessmen, and the new company was proud of its first steamer. The PRINCE CADWGAN had been built for them by the Union Shipbuilding Company, Kelvinhaugh, who built her in an extremely robust fashion. Despite her enormous strength of clinker construction on iron frames, she nevertheless leaked a lot and was continually in need of repairs, often taking all the shareholders annual profits to keep her afloat. One example of PRINCE CADWGAN'S unfortunate breakdowns was in 1872 when her propeller shaft broke in the trunk when she was off St Govan's Head. However, she survived this mishap unscathed. The steamer regularly traded with Bristol and it was on her return from that port that she met her fate.

Returning from Bristol with a general cargo, including iron and petroleum, the PRINCE CADWGAN was leaving Solva in darkness on the last day of September 1876. It was very early in the morning and and as she steamed for the entrance to Ramsey Sound, her propeller hit a submerged rock. The surprise was presumably Half-Tide Rock, an unexpected outcrop which as its name implies only shows itself at low water.

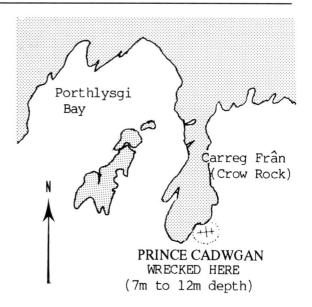

PRINCE CADWGAN
WRECKED HERE
(7m to 12m depth)

The collision took the blades clean off her propeller. In a disabled condition the PRINCE CADWGAN was blown onto the nearby rocks where she was holed and sank in shallow water. Captain Thomas Evans and all the crew got safely ashore and were looked after by the farmer at Treginnis.

It was a sad end to Aberaeron's first steamer and led to the dissolution of the Aberayron Steam Navigation Company Ltd. However the port was not long without a steamer for the following year a new company, The Aberayron Steam Packet Company, was formed with the IANTHE steamer which proved to be much a more profitable investment for the shareholders.

PRINCESS IRENE

Type: Cargo Steamer, Steel Screw
Port of Registry: Glasgow
Official Number: 98602
Tonnage: 763 tons register
Built: 1891, Dundee
Length: 209 feet
Breadth: 30 feet
Date of Sinking: August 20th 1906
Location: Linney Head, Pembrokeshire, Dyfed

The PRINCESS IRENE set out from Aberdeen on August 17th with a mixed cargo for Bristol. She soon met with thick fog and her Captain had to navigate with extra care. The steamer passed the lighthouse of the Smalls and her course was then altered to enter the Bristol Channel. It was this course that caused her undoing, like many steamers before her, due allowance was not made for the north-going tidal stream.

As the ship steamed towards St Govan's Head the tide took her a few miles further north than her intended course. Instead of rounding St Govan's Head she drove straight into Linney Head, a head on collision with the rocks in the dense fog.

The Board of Trade cliff rescue team went to help and the crew were safely landed using the rocket apparatus. They all waited until low water so that they could return to get their belongings and the ship's papers.

The Western Mail two days later gave the following report; 'Messrs Langlands of Liverpool have received a telegram announcing that their Glasgow steamer PRINCESS IRENE went on the rocks in the fog at Linney Head, Pembrokeshire, on Monday night on a voyage from Aberdeen to Bristol. There is little hope of saving the steamer, her engine room and hold being flooded and her hull torn in several places. Her Captain also reports that the vessel's back is broken, and there is little hope of doing anything for her. The deck cargo is being washed away. All the crew are reported safe'.

Two weeks later various items salvaged from the PRINCESS IRENE were auctioned at Milford Docks. Goods sold included oils, beer, whisky, soap, candles, canvas and ropes. Some articles salvaged from the wreck did not get to the sale, these included nicely perfumed soaps and sandals with rope soles. So many rope sandals were distributed among the local people that the comment was made that you could tell which village people came from by the summer footwear they wore.

PRINCESS IRENE breaking up on the rocks near Linney Head, Pembrokeshire after stranding there in a thick fog in 1906.
Photo: Roger Worsley Collection

RAGNA

Type: Sailing Ship, 3 Masted Barque
Port of Registry: Kristiansand, Norway
Previous Name: HILDA
Tonnage: 718 tons
Built: 1878, New Glasgow, Nova Scotia
Length: 162 feet
Breadth: 34 feet
Date of Sinking: December 28th 1900
Location: Trefin, Pembrokeshire, Dyfed

A hurricane from the north west started to blow on Thursday, December 27th 1900. This severe storm was to cause chaos around the entire coastline in the next twenty four hours. Steamers going north, up the Irish Sea, were incapable of making any headway and the weather was so appalling that many sailing vessels had little chance of survival. One of the casualties was the barque RAGNA, outward bound from Cardiff with a cargo of coal for Bahia, Argentina.

In the tremendous storm the RAGNA found herself dragging her anchors outside the little bay of Aberfelin, about eight miles north of St David's Head. The barque, being fully laden and exposed to the full force of the sea, was doomed.

The RAGNA dragged towards the cliffs and in twenty minutes was grinding and breaking up on the rocks. The villagers all rushed down to the bay to help, one of them braced himself on the cliff above and captured the dramatic scene on his camera. The photograph shows the distressed vessel moments before her masts toppled. It is a remarkable photograph considering the appalling difficulties for the photographer. The crew were still aboard deciding how to get to the shore. Men from Trefin, especially Mr Thomas and William Mathias, were successful in getting long lengths of rope across to the wreck which helped some of the crew escape.

The men on board could not launch the lifeboats as the waves breaking over the decks were too rough. Some of the crew jumped overboad and managed to get ashore by dragging themselves through the surf on the ropes that the people on the shore had secured. Others tried to swim ashore unaided. One man jumped over the port side of the wreck and was trying to swim for the shore when the main mast toppled and struck him in the water. He was killed instantly and a further 8 men were lost.

Captain Zopfie, who commanded the RAGNA was amongst the survivors and many of his crew were badly cut and injured from being thrown against the rocks. The bodies of three crewmen washed ashore and they were buried together in the new cemetery at Llanrian. The local people were not only totally involved in the rescue, provided comfort and care for the survivors, but also donated an impressive tombstone for the grave of the three lost sailors.

A sailor who made the crossing from Milford to Waterford decribes the fury of the sea that night: 'The weather was terrific. I have been seventeen years knocking about the world; I have seen the waves running pretty high about Cape Horn, but I never saw a sea like the one in the Channel on Thursday night!'

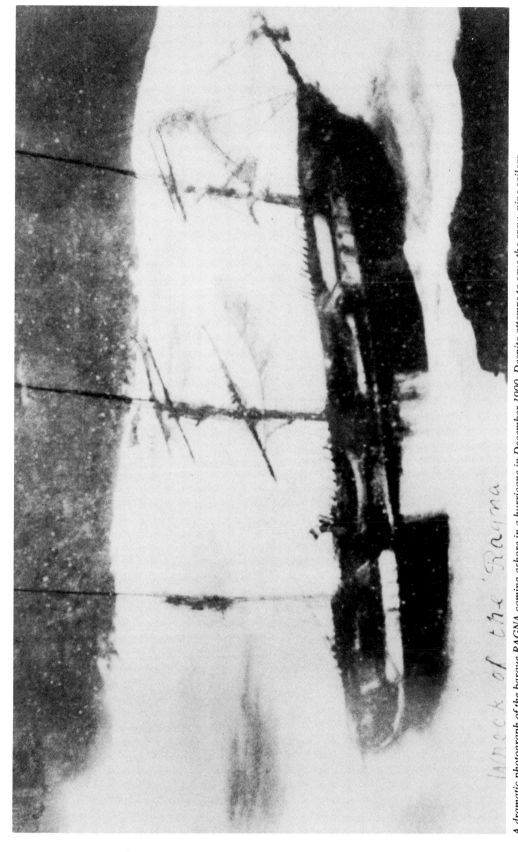

Wreck of the Ragna

A dramatic photograph of the barque RAGNA coming ashore in a hurricane in December 1900. Despite attemps to save the crew, nine sailors were being swept by the seas to their deaths while this photograph was being taken.

Photo: Courtesy of the Ship Inn, Trefin

Over 130 local subscribers contributed to the burial expenses and the cost of this impressive tombstone for the three foreign sailors lost when the RAGNA was wrecked at Trefin, North Pembrokeshire

Photo: John Bennett

RESURGAM

Type: Submarine, experimental
Tonnage: 30 ton displacement
Built: 1879, Birkenhead
Length: 42 feet
Breadth: 9 feet
Depth: 12 feet
Engine: Lamm latent heat steam engine
Date of Sinking: February 25th 1880
Location: Off Llandudno, Gwynedd

A brilliant and eccentric curate from Manchester was one of the first inventors to build a full size mechanically powered submarine. The submarine was cylindrically shaped with cone shaped ends, built of iron and girthed with half a metre of timber she was constructed by J.T. Cochran & Company at Birkenhead in 1879 at a cost of £1,538. Successful initial trials in Alfred Dock convinced the Admiralty that they were interested in the invention and wished to see the new craft for trials at the Royal Naval base at Gosport.

Ignoring advice to transport the submarine by train to Portsmouth the inventor, 27 year old Reverend George W. Garrett, B.A., stubbonly decided to take her there by sea. With the help of two friends he started out on December 10th 1879, and such was his faith in his submarine that he left without any escort. The first night they spent entirely submerged and for a greater part of the next three days they remained in the submarine with the hatch locked down. While travelling, the three men were subject to the discomfort of high humidity, intense temperatures and lack of space to lie down. The Lamm steam engine was designed on the principle that once enough head of steam had been produced, the boiler fire could be extinguished allowing the engine to continue turning the propeller for a few hours while in the submerged state. The main difficulty for Pastor Garrett and his crew was one of overcoming temperatures of 43 degrees centigrade while inside the RESURGAM as it slowly moved along the north Wales coast at less than walking pace. After three days in the hot cramped conditions, and having to remain permanently upright in an internal diameter of only two metres, the men came ashore at Rhyl, somewhat exhausted. They found lodgings to get a good night's sleep.

For the following month they based themselves in the River Clwyd while further tests and adaptions were made to the submarine. Pastor Garrett realized that an escort boat was needed to accompany the RESURGAM on her trip, so a steam yacht named ELFIN was called for. The voyage was resumed on the night of February 24th with ELFIN towing the submarine towards Llandudno. Within 24 hours a gale from the west north west hit them and the RESURGAM, with no crew aboard, broke loose from the tow, never to be seen again.

The name RESURGAM means 'I shall rise again' and that is the aspiration of Bill Garrett, the great grandson of the inventor who is hopeful of recovering the submarine and for her to be displayed at the Royal Naval Submarine Museum at Gosport. During 1989, he searched for the RESURGAM but, like other expeditions since 1975, the submarine's location remained a mystery. Perhaps by the time this book is published she will rise again and continue her journey to Gosport after 111 years beneath the waves.

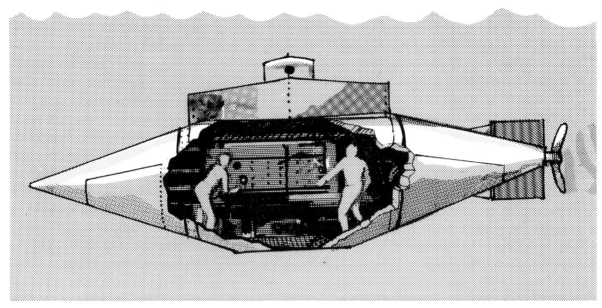

Author's illustration of the experimental submarine RESURGAM, showing the inventor and his colleague in the cramped interior

Although unrelated to any specific shipwreck story in this book, the following extract was found within the pages of a Welsh newspaper and amused the author enough to include it here.

One of the passengers on board an ill fated vessel at the time of a wreck was an exceedingly nervous man. Finding himself in the water he imagined what his friends would do to acquaint his wife with his fate. Saved at last, he rushed to the telegraph office and sent this message.

'DEAR P., I AM SAVED.
BREAK IT GENTLY TO MY WIFE.'

(Cambrian newspaper, October 28th 1881)

RHOSNEIGR

Type: Passenger Paddle Steamer
Port of Registry: Southampton
Official Number: 72361
Previous Name: PRINCE LEOPOLD
Tonnage: 196 tons gross
Built: 1876, Glasgow
Length: 165 feet
Breadth: 20 feet
Engines: 70 nhp
Date of Sinking: July 20th 1908
Location: Rhos on Sea, Colwyn Bay, Clwyd

Captain Walter Hawthorn of Rhyl purchased the RHOSNEIGR in June 1908, with the intention of running the paddle steamer on trips between Llandudno and Rhos on Sea. His venture with this vessel was short lived because she sank off Rhos Pier just one month later.

Built in 1876 and named PRINCE LEOPOLD, she started out as a passenger ferry between the Isle of Wight and Southampton. Capable of 12 knots and carrying 463 passengers she commenced service with the Colwyn Bay and Liverpool Steamship Company in 1905.

On her last trip she was carrying passengers on a pleasure trip from Llandudno to Blackpool and back, cost 2/6d (12p). The paddle steamer was nearing Rhos Pier to pick up more passengers when water suddenly poured into her hull.

Captain Smallman ordered all bulkheads to be closed as he tried to continue but a quarter of a mile from the Pier it was obvious that he was not going to make it. With continuous blasting of the the ship's siren he drove the sinking RHOSNEIGR directly towards the shore where she grounded. There were only two lifeboats aboard the paddle steamer, but using these and a further two from her sister ship, the RHOS TREVOR, conveniently anchored nearby, all the passengers were successfully ferried ashore.

On the rising tide the RHOSNEIGR refloated briefly, then sank quickly by the stern, sending her new owner into the water. He fortunately survived but the paddle steamer did not. The RHOSNEIGR broke up and left her jagged pieces of ironwork rotting on the lower foreshore for the next sixty years.

ROCHE CASTLE

Type: Steam Trawler
Port of Registry: Swansea
Official Number: 143995
Tonnage: 307 tons
Built: 1938, Selby
Length: 130 feet
Breadth: 24 feet
Engines: Triple 3 cylinder, 91 nhp
Date of Sinking: January 10th 1937
Location: Near Overton, Gower, Glamorgan

James Insole, Skipper of the Swansea trawler ROCHE CASTLE was returning home with a full load of fish caught off the south west coast of Ireland when he came upon fog in the Bristol Channel. Together with his ten all Welsh crew, he continued; the nearer he got to Swansea the thicker the fog became.

With an almighty crash, they hit the coast a few miles west of his home port. Immediately an S.O.S was sent out and by 10pm the Mumbles Lifeboat was on its way. With an ebbing tide the Lifeboat was unable to get close enough to help those aboard. The Lifeboat stood by until 5am and Skipper Insole was still hopeful that he would be able to get his trawler off the rocks. This was not to be, at high water the stranded vessel was rocked violently by a big swell and it was obvious that they had to abandon via a breeches buoy that had been rigged up by the Rhossili team.

Great problems were experienced keeping proper tension on the rescue line and as the first man was pulled ashore in the breeches buoy, another crewman, George Gaylor, also tried to hang on. With the slackening and tension on the line as the trawler rocked to and fro, the line threw the second man into the sea and he was drowned.

It was a difficult rescue but the remainder of the crew got ashore, Skipper Insole being the last to leave. They were met on the cliff top by about one hundred and fifty people and with lanterns they made their way over rough ground to Overton Farm where they were cared for and given hot drinks.

Skipper Insole remarked 'It was a big relief when we were drawn through the surf to land. When we reached the shore the farmers and others were very kind to us. It is a wonder that anybody was saved.'

It was an extremely difficult rescue and all those involved were commended for their actions by the owners and the Board of Trade.

The ROCHE CASTLE, a Swansea Trawler, smashing into the cliffs of the Gower. A brilliant rescue saved all but one of the crew.
Photo: Courtesy of Mrs A. Hughes

STEEPHOLM

Type: Motor Vessel, Sand Dredger
Port of Registry: Bristol
Built: 1950, Bristol
Tonnage: 532 tons
Length: 150 feet
Breadth: 31 feet
Date of Sinking: October 3rd 1968
Location: Tusker Rock, Porthcawl, Glamorgan

The Bristol sand dredger STEEPHOLM had spent her life plying the shallow waters of the Bristol Channel sucking up sand for her owners the Holms Sand and Gravel Company. Her loss in 1968 was in waters that were well known to her Captain but it was a series of mishaps that caused her to hit the Tusker Rock after the ship's pumping equipment and lighting failed. It was severe weather when the STEEPHOLM got into trouble on a voyage from Bristol to Swansea and she was soon driven towards Porthcawl where the waves were breaking five metres high at the seafront.

The stricken ship hit the notorious reef of Tusker Rock and with the dredger grounding heavily on the rock the crew inflated the liferafts and abandoned her. The Captain remained on board to send out Mayday messages although it seemed that at any moment the vessel would break apart.

The Mumbles Lifeboat arrived on the scene in the nick of time. The lifeline attaching one of the liferafts to the dredger had just parted and the raft was rapidly drifting away. After picking up the 6 crew the Lifeboat returned to the wreck which was by now listing badly and in danger of breaking up. The Captain was still aboard and Coxswain Scott manoeuvred the bow of the Lifeboat into the dredger's deck which was awash. The Captain plunged into the sea and managed, by the tips of his fingers, to reach the edge of the Lifeboat and he was hauled aboard.

The weather was atrocious with thick mist, a rough sea and heavy rain and the STEEPHOLM remained upright and firm on the rock. The following day the Dutch salvage tug UTRECHT, which was equipped with all the latest salvage equipment and had been involved with the TORRY CANYON drama the year before, was quickly on site and stood by in case she was needed. When it became obvious that the dredger was beyond repair the salvage tug departed.

The STEEPHOLM broke up on the east end of the Tusker, the seas smashing her into three seperate portions. Her remains are now disintegrating into the sands of the Bristol Channel which were such an important part of her life.

The author remembers as a boy spending a day out from Bristol aboard this vessel while she went about her business of collecting sand near Flatholm and can vividly remember the fascination of seeing odd coins screened out of the sand in mid- Channel possibly washed out from the beaches of Barry or Weston Super Mare.

The STEEPHOLM on Tusker Rock, Porthcawl prior to her breaking into three pieces
Photos: Tony Comley

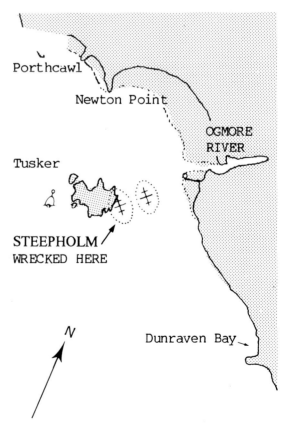

DIVE DETAILS

Location: 51° 26' 50" N   03° 39' 17" W approx.
On the east end of Tusker Rock, broken into
three pieces.
Depth: 2m to 7m
Seabed: sand, rock and silt
Currents: strong
Visibility: poor
Launch Site: Porthcawl

STRATHALLAN

Type: Cargo Steamer
Port of Registry: Glasgow
Official Number: 84303
Tonnage: 410 tons register
Built: 1881, Glasgow
Date of Sinking: March 29th 1887
Location: Off Lavernock Point, Glamorgan

The Glasgow steamer STRATHALLAN had loaded with a full cargo of 720 tons of Welsh coal at Cardiff and was outward bound to the French port of St Malo. The pilot left the vessel when they were off Penarth and the Master, Samuel Henry Park, was well aware that to make a good start on his journey he must take full advantage of the ebb tide out of the Bristol Channel. With the strong tide in his favour he ordered full steam and pushed on into the dark and hazy night, at full speed. It was a decision for which he would be severely criticised.

Captain Park was at the helm and with a three and a half knot current in his favour he steamed at full speed between Raines Buoy and Lavernock Point. The Chief Mate and an able seaman were on lookout when two lights were seen ahead. The brighter of the two lights was an anchored barque and the other, much dimmer, was an anchored steamer. The helm was starboarded but the anchored steamer was much nearer than they had expected and there was no time to avoid a collision. There was an almighty crash as the STRATHALLAN collided with the stern of the anchored steamer that was twice her size. The STRATHALLAN'S six year old hull was ripped open near the bow and she heeled over to starboard and sank in about three minutes. Before the boat could be got out, all were in the water. Besides the 13 crew, there was one Swansea passenger and there was some suspicion as to whether a stowaway was also aboard. 8 of the crew were saved and 5 were lost, and if there had been a stowaway, 6 lives would have been lost.

The steamer she had hit was the 1,304 ton ADALA of Shoreham, which was temporarily anchored near the West Cardiff Buoy. The ADALA herself had an hour earlier had a minor collision with an anchored schooner and the ADALA's Captain had stopped to assess if damage had been done to both his ship and that of the schooner. The ADALA had anchored and put up her anchor lights and shortly after was hit by the STRATHALLAN.

The subsequent Court of Inquiry considered that Captain Park was to blame for the loss of his vessel stating that the STRATHALLAN was going too fast, and was being driven in a reckless manner with no proper regard taken of the strength of the outgoing tide.

SZENT ISTVAN

Type: Cargo Steamship
Port of Registry: Fiume/Rijeka, Croatia
Code Letters: JSFM
Tonnage: 2,215 tons gross, 1,376 tons net
Built: 1892, Newcastle
Length: 285 feet
Breadth: 38 feet
Engines: Triple Expansion, Steam, 237 nhp
Date of Sinking: September 28th 1908
Location: Ramsey Island, Pembrokeshire, Dyfed

The largest steamer to hit the rocks of Ramsey Island was the GRAFFOE (see Volume 1) in 1905, three years later a cargo steamer, almost as big, crashed into the southern corner of the island.

The details of Monday morning in September 1908 are best recalled by Ivor Arnold, who was farming, by himself, on the island. In his diary he wrote;

'Wind South blowing and very foggy. I was alone on the island. At 2am Monday the Austro-Hungarian steamship (SZENT ISTVAN) of Fiume, struck and sank off the SW of Ramsey island in a place called Slippery Hill. The SS SZENT ISTVAN had 3,500 tons of general cargo mostly flour and had a crew of 27 men. I was chopping up sticks in the house when three men came to the door at 7am. They had a hatchet and a long knife in their hands, which I couldn't help keeping my eyes on. They were jabbering something which I couldn't understand, so I brought them an Atlas and they pointed out Fiume in Austria and from there to Lisbon and then Ramsey. I came to the conclusion they were shipwrecked on the island. These three men landed (Abermawr) and lost their boat. I went out with them to look for the rest of the crew and found them about 10am. They had landed (in the NE corner of the island) and moored their three boats there. The men had lost everything. I gave them tea and two loaves of bread 1lb. butter which included all I had. They ate it ravenously, though sad to say some of the youngest boys had none. They stopped in St David's for several days. They were lodged and boarded by the Shipwreck Society. I piloted them across the Sound to St Justinian in their own boats. Miss Baker (Justinian) received them on the Lifeboat slip and showed them every kindness. This young lady gave them warm tea and milk and helped them in addressing letters and writing telegrams'.

Part of the SZENT ISTVAN'S hull was visible above the waves for a week but conditions were too hazardous to make a serious attempt at salvaging the cargo, intended for Glasgow, worth an estimated £200,000.

Boats laid up for the winter at St David's, Solva and Little Haven were hurriedly launched in order to see what wreckage was about. A lot of the flour cargo washed onto the beaches and people collected what they could in all sorts of containers including pillowcases. Everyone was so preoccupied with walking the beaches or being afloat to see what could be salvaged that the local newspaper commented that the Churches were only half full that Sunday and that people were more interested in wrecking than attending Church.

How to locate the SZENT ISTVAN

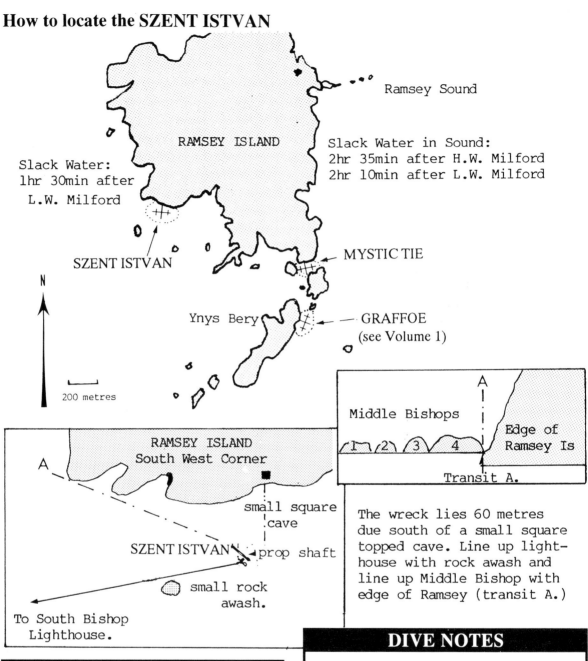

Ramsey Sound

RAMSEY ISLAND

Slack Water in Sound:
2hr 35min after H.W. Milford
2hr 10min after L.W. Milford

Slack Water:
1hr 30min after
L.W. Milford

SZENT ISTVAN

N

MYSTIC TIE

Ynys Bery

GRAFFOE
(see Volume 1)

200 metres

Middle Bishops

Edge of
Ramsey Is

1 2 3 4

Transit A.

RAMSEY ISLAND
South West Corner

A

small square
cave

SZENT ISTVAN

prop shaft

small rock
awash.

To South Bishop
Lighthouse.

The wreck lies 60 metres
due south of a small square
topped cave. Line up lighthouse with rock awash and
line up Middle Bishop with
edge of Ramsey (transit A.)

DIVE NOTES

This has been a popular diving site for the last
decade and the wreck is dispersed over a large
area of the seabed. Even if you are not interested
in seeing ironwork underwater it is an interesting
place to dive and the author has seen seals
underwater here. Atlantic seals may be
troublesome in the Autumn, especially the bulls.
Take a marker buoy (SMB) in the event of the
dive becoming a drift dive.

DIVE DETAILS

Location: 51° 51' 25" N   05° 20' 54" W
On the South West corner of Ramsey Island
Depth: 11m to 22m
Seabed: rock & boulders
Currents: manageable but strong nearby
Underwater Visibility: good
Launch site: Porthclais or Porthgain

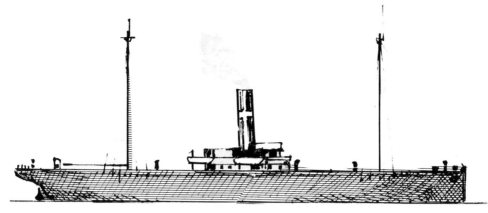

Author's illustration of the SZENT ISTVAN lost on Ramsey Island in 1909

Artefacts recovered from the wreck site:
Ship's taffrail log
Ship's gimballed chronometer
Part of the letter 'E' of the nameplate from the SZENT ISTVAN.
Photos: Courtesy of P.A. Mack and members of the Manchester Diving Group

TIMBO

Type: Cargo Steamship
Port of Registry: Whitby
Official Number: 89765
Tonnage: 295 tons gross
Built: 1883, Newcastle
Length: 145 feet
Breadth: 20 feet
Engines: 60 rhp
Date of Rescue: December 3rd 1920
Location: Caernarfon Bay, Gwynedd

Nine lives were lost in the winter storm of 1920 in the waters near Caernarfon Bar. It was an incident that shocked the people of Rhoscolyn. They lost five of their most able Lifeboatmen and as a consequence, some nine years later, the village found it impossible to provide sufficient Lifeboatmen to serve the lifeboat and the station was closed.

It was December 1920, a hurricane of great force swept across Ireland, Wales, Northern England and Scotland. It brought thunder, lightning, lashings of rain and eighty mile an hour winds. The weather caused loss of life on land, but it was far worse at sea. The iron screw steamer TIMBO was rounding Anglesey on a voyage from her home port of Liverpool to Newport,

The TIMBO aground in 1920
Photo: Henry Parry Collection, Gwynedd Archives Services

A rowing lifeboat being battered by waves on its way to a wreck. The 13 man crew of the Rhoscolyn Lifeboat had similar conditions to this when 5 of them were washed away.
Etching: Tom Bennett Collection

Gwent, when she was driven towards the bar at Caernarfon. The steamer carried an 8 man crew and the Rhoscolyn Lifeboat set out to assist.

The ferocious waves and surf in the shallow waters were too much for a rowing Lifeboat. As the TIMBO was holding on her anchors the Lifeboat Coxswain, Owen Owens, decided to row for the shelter of Llanddwyn. The lifeboat crew had been at sea for about an hour when a big wave swept off two of the Lifeboat's 13 crew. Some time later a second disaster struck, the Lifeboat was thrown on its beam ends with the loss of three more men.

Meanwhile those on board the TIMBO, seeing no hope of being rescued, made the fateful mistake of launching one of their own lifeboats, manned by five men, this was overwhelmed and four were drowned.

The TIMBO broke away from her two anchors and ended up high and dry on the shingle beach at Dinas Dinlle, causing little damage to her hull. The Captain and the remaining members of the crew were saved. After the building of a launching ramp and a complicated salvage operation, the TIMBO was refloated.

Coxswain Owen Owens was one of the five Lifeboatmen who lost his life and all five were buried together at Rhoscolyn churchyard.

TIVYSIDE

Type: Coastal Steamer
Port of Registry: Liverpool
Official Number: 63367
Tonnage: 125 tons gross
Built: 1869, Glasgow
Length: 115 feet
Breadth: 18 feet
Engines: Compound 2 cylinder, 25 hp
Date of Sinking: June 14th 1900
Location: Overton, Gower, Glamorgan

Not to be outdone by their neighbours in Aberaeron, the Cardigan merchants decided in 1868 to form their own company and to have a trading steamer that would do similar trade to the Aberayron Steam Packet Company's steamer PRINCE CADWGAN.

An order was made for a steamer to be built with the London and Glasgow Engineering and Iron Shipbuilding Company and when it arrived in Cardigan in August 1869 it caused great excitement in the town. The steamer was aptly named TIVYSIDE although it is curious that the first owner was Thomas Davies and Company, Thomas Davies being the biggest timber merchant in the town and, chairman of the newly formed Cardigan Steam Navigation Company. The vessel was not officially registered in the name of the company until 1885.

The vessel was strongly built of iron, with an original tonnage of 108 tons gross, 53 tons net and 100 feet long, she could steam at 9 to 10 knots without a cargo which was impressive for a small 2 cylinder engine of only 25 horsepower. The Tivyside Advertiser in 1882 comments 'On April 21st the steamer TIVYSIDE left Bristol at 4 pm and was alongside her discharging wharf at Cardigan next morning at 7.35am. Very good steaming!'

In 1888 the TIVYSIDE was owned by Thomas Jenkins of Carmarthen who sold it to the Liverpool firm of John Bacon Limited in 1895. One year later she was lengthened to 115 feet and her tonnage increased to 125 tons gross. The charming photograph of her alongside at Bristol is of the TIVYSIDE in her lengthened state.

Her loss is reported in the South Wales Daily News dated June 16th 1900.

'Yesterday morning information reached Swansea that the SS TIVYSIDE had gone ashore off Porteynon during the night, but the crew had been saved. Her crew numbered 6 all told, her Skipper being Captain Harvey, of Liverpool. The Chief Engineer hails from Carmarthen, but there are no other South Walians among the crew. It is assumed that the steering gear went wrong and that this caused her to go on the rocks'.

It was also reported that the crew saved themselves in their own boats and that the vessel was badly holed on the rocks at Overton Cliffs.

It was the first and last trading steamer to be owned by the Cardigan Steam Navigation Company.

The Cardigan steamer TIVYSIDE alongside the quay at Bristol
Photo: Bristol City Museum & Welsh Industrial & Maritime Museum

TRIDONIA

Type: Sailing Ship, 3 Masted Barque
Port of Registry: London
Previous Names: JEAN BART, HEINZ
Tonnage: 2,224 tons gross
Built: 1901, St Nazaire, Brittany
Length: 281 feet
Breadth: 40 feet
Date of Sinking: October 30th 1916
Location: Oxwich Bay, Gower, Glamorgan

The last of the square-rigged sailing ships to be wrecked on the South Wales coast was the TRIDONIA in 1916. Built of steel in 1901 at St Nazaire she was named JEAN BART, but later in her life was renamed HEINZ when she came under German ownership. In August 1914 when World War 1 was declared she happened to be a German ship in British waters and was immediately interned.

Renamed TRIDONIA and under the command of Captain Stewart this large sailing ship set out from Belfast to collect a cargo of grain from the River Plate. On her outward journey she met with Atlantic storms which caused her to return to the shelter of Cork. On setting out once more she met even worse weather which blew away most of her sails and she was swept back into the Bristol Channel in a dishevelled state. The pilot, W.J.Davies, was put aboard and the barque attempted to ride out the storm in Porteynon Bay. In the late afternoon both anchor cables parted as the heavy gale tore at the chains at low water. She hit the rocky platform bows-on, in a spot not far from where the DUISBERG (see Volume 1) had come ashore 17 years earlier.

Darkness fell and the storm force winds did not abate as the tide rose. Four of the crew launched the ship's boat in an attempt to get a line to the shore. The boat was swamped but the men were helped ashore by people wading out to them in the surf. The remaining crew, the Captain and his wife spent a miserable night sheltering as best they could inside makeshift tents made from the remnants of the torn sails lashed to the jib-boom.

The Mumbles Lifeboat failed to reach the scene and the Tenby Lifeboat got to within 100 metres of the wreck but was then forced away by the seas without saving any of them. Throughout the night members of both the Oxwich Lifesaving Company and the Rhossili team persisted in a desperate effort to fire rocket lines out to the ship.

94

The TRIDONIA'S decks were continually being swept by waves and during the night the Captain, Second Mate and a Lascar seaman were tragically washed overboard and lost.

By morning all were astonished to see that the masts were still standing and that a rocket fired by the Rhossili rocket crew had actually gone over the ship unnoticed. A breeches buoy was rigged up and subsequently brought ashore Mrs Stewart, 20 crew and the pilot. All were cold, shocked and fatigued including some members of the rocket crew that had been helping on the cliffs for 30 hours. The TRIDONIA quickly broke apart.

As the last of the crew were being taken off the wreck they took pity on 3 pigs that were still aboard. The pigs were promptly thrown overboard and they were forced to swim ashore to survive. This they managed to do without much trouble but then were kept in quarantine for three months.

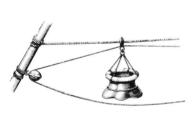

Etchings showing how rocket line is fired out to a wreck and the landing of the crew by Breeches Buoy
Illustrations: Tom Bennett Collection

TWELVE APOSTLES

Type: Sailing Vessel, Schooner Rigged
Port of Registry: Porthmadog
Tonnage: 118 tons net
Built: 1858, Pwllheli
Length: 82 feet
Breadth: 22 feet
Date of Sinking: November 23rd 1898
Location: Hell's Mouth, near Pwllheli, Gwynedd

Great symbolism was made of the fact that the TWELVE APOSTLES (a Porthmadog Schooner) was swallowed up in a part of Cardigan Bay known as Hell's Mouth; an area not far from St Patrick's Causeway.

Built at Pwllheli, the schooner was so named by a religious merchant from the Baltic, where it regularly traded. Having given the Stettin businessman the honour of choosing a name, his odd choice could not be refused considering his devout Lutheran views. Owned by H.Hughes and others and with Captain John James Jones as master, the vessel survived forty years and was one of the last sail trading ships of the port. The schooner, with her figurehead of a bust of St Paul, was said to be the unofficial flagship of Porthmadog. She was often seen lying at the quayside flying a silk burgee with the Twelve Apostles painted upon it.

The November gale in 1898 brought havoc to the waters of Cardigan Bay, damage to at least three Porthmadog vessels and a Scottish brigantine was lost with all hands. Captain Richard Jones,

John James Jones's brother of Borth y Gest, was at the helm of the TWELVE APOSTLES and he took the brave decision to run the vessel ashore in order to save the ship and the crew. His plan did not work but he did manage to get himself and his crew to the shore with the aid of the ship's boat and help from a servant girl who waded into the surf to save them.

A telegram was sent to the owners in Porthmadog with the message, 'Twelve Apostles making water in Hell's Mouth', a statement that prompted spirited conversation long after the event.

S. S. VALSESIA. WRECKED ON BARRY ISLAND

This large Italian steamer bringing American coal to Barry ran aground at Friars Point in 1926, and became a total loss
Photo: Tom Bennett Collection

VALSESIA

Type: Cargo Steamer
Port of Registry: Genoa, Italy
Previous Name: PIOMBINO II
Tonnage: 6,606 tons gross
Built: 1922, Piombino
Length: 397 feet
Breadth: 53 feet
Engines: Turbines steam
Date of Sinking: August 25th 1926
Location: Friar's Point, Barry, Glamorgan

A large Italian steamer stranded at Friars Point provided an unusual spectacle for the thousands of holiday makers who were at Barry Island in August 1926. The vessel was the VALSESIA which was taking a cargo of 7,700 tons of American coal to Barry Docks, due to the coal strike in South Wales.

The VALSESIA ran ashore at Friars Point and although two tugs quickly got to her they failed to tow her off before the tide receded. That evening the tugs made a second attempt, with the VALSESIA'S bow well up the rocks her stern swung round and, she slipped into deeper water. The Cardiff tugs PRAIRIE FLOWER and BANTAMCOCK towed her towards the centre of Whitmore Bay, but their efforts were in vain, the men on the bows of the VALSESIA could not release the anchor chain. This had the effect of pulling the ship back to her original position.

On the outgoing tide it was noticed that the VALSESIA had broken her back and it was feared she might split in two. At low water people could walk on the sands around the wreck and at high water a fortune was made by the boat trip operators conveying tourists to look at her.

In the middle of the night the Barry Signal Station played a powerful searchlight on the wreck and hundreds of people watched, every few minutes they could hear clearly the grinding of the VALSESIA'S hull as it scraped the rocks.

Oxy-acetylene burning gear was brought to the site and holes were cut in the VALSESIA's hull to scuttle her in that position. The wreck and her cargo was valued at £75,000. Eventually she split in two and was abandoned on the beach. In January, W.Thomas Ward Limited bought the wreck for £6,600 (£1 per ton), and in March the two halves were towed to the scrap yard at Briton Ferry.

VERNICOS ALEXIA

Type: Tug
Port of Registry: Piraeus, Greece
Official Number: 183813
Previous Names: FORMBY, WEATHER
           COCK
Tonnage: 237 tons gross
Built: 1951, Selby
Length: 109 feet
Breadth: 26 feet
Engines: Oil, T 3 Cy. 1,088 bhp
Date of Sinking: October 18th 1981
Location: Near Solva, Pembrokeshire, Dyfed

VERNICOS GEORGOS

Type: Tug
Port of Registry: Piraeus, Greece
Official Number: 183812
Previous Names: CANADA II, CANADA,
           PEA COCK
Tonnage: 237 tons gross
Built: 1951, Selby
Length: 109 feet
Breadth: 26 feet
Engines: Oil, T 3 Cy. 1,088 bhp
Date of Sinking: October 18th 1981
Location: Near Solva, Pembrokeshire, Dyfed

VERNICOS BARBARA IV

Type: Tug
Port of Registry: Piraeus, Greece
Previous Names: COLLINGWOOD II,
           COLLINGWOOD,
           HEATH COCK
Built: 1958 to 1960, Birkenhead
Length: 95 feet
Breadth: 26 feet
Engines: Oil, 1,088 bhp
Date of Sinking: October 18th 1981
Location: Near Solva, Pembrokeshire, Dyfed

In 1981 the Greek Vernicos Company purchased three secondhand Mersey tugs from the Alexandra Towing Company Ltd. of Liverpool who had acquired them from the Liverpool Screw Towing Company in 1966. In October 1981, only five months after the purchase, a series of unfortunate events occurred which caused them to lose all three of their newly acquired vessels.

The tugs were on passage from Liverpool to Piraeus. It was decided that one tug should tow the other two on the first leg of the trip from Liverpool to Appledore. The tug chosen to do the tow was the VERNICOS GEORGOS (ex CANADA II) which, for the previous two years, had been stationed at Great Yarmouth.

All went according to plan until the three tug party arrived off St David's. The towing tug developed engine trouble. They stopped to deal with the problem in the approaches to St Bride's Bay. When they recommenced the tow the eight hundred metre towrope became fouled around the single screw propeller of the VERNICOS GEORGOS, the towing vessel.

A fast inflatable with divers went out from Solva to help but they were given erroneous bearings and they failed to find the tugs or see any lights. The weather deteriorated and all three tugs came ashore on the rocks three quarters of a mile west of Solva.

The 8 man crew was rescued by the combined operation of the H M Coastguard, R A F Brawdy and the St David's Lifeboat. 3 men from the VERNICOS GEORGOS were rescued by the Lifeboat which later hit bottom and backed off. A Sea King helicopter from 202 Squadron, Brawdy, airlifted the remaining crew members.

It was an unusual scenario in that three, almost identical, vessels were stranded simultaneously to become total losses.

VERNICOS GEORGOS was the first to split apart and within a few months was embedded in bits amongst the lower tide line. The VERNICOS ALEXIA landing higher up the same beach took a few years to break apart and the VERNICOS BARBARA IV, being in a relatively sheltered spot on the next beach, was still in a recognisable condition after five years. These remains have provided a lot of interest to those walking the Pembrokeshire Coast Path and are a modern day reminder of how shipwrecks happen as well as showing us the destructive power of waves.

Engine parts of one of the tugs now to be seen scattered on the beach near Solva ten years after the stranding
Photo: Tom Bennett

A triple calamity, the three Vernicos tugs lie awash near Solva in October 1981
Photo: David Owen

WAPELLA

Type: Sailing Ship, Barque Rigged
Port of Registry: New Orleans
Tonnage: 728 tons register
Date of Sinking: January 25th 1868
Location: Dyffryn, near Barmouth, Gwynedd

The WAPELLA was an American sailing ship, cotton laden and ending an Atlantic crossing when she fell prey to the shallow waters of Cardigan Bay. The scenario was to be repeated many times during the Victorian era. The ship, with a cargo intended for the Lancashire mills, missed her course for Liverpool and, having once strayed into Cardigan Bay was trapped at Sarn Badrig (St Patrick's Causeway), a rocky reef that extends some miles out to sea.

On this occasion the ship had left New Orleans with a cargo of cotton, staves and oil cake and carried a crew of 12 with 3 passengers including a young German boy. The Captain, Isaac Orr, the Mate and 3 seamen were from Bath, Maine. Other seamen were from Liverpool, Ireland, Scotland and Sweden and, curiously, one of the passengers was Ellen Watkins of Beaumaris.

The WAPELLA missed her course for Liverpool and became embayed in Cardigan Bay, a gale blew up and drove the barque on to the beach at Dyffryn, near Barmouth. It was 10 o'clock on a fierce dark mid-winter's night and those on board had not the least idea as to where they were.

They remained on board throughout the night and an hour before dawn got into three of the ship's longboats. They remained at the stern of the vessel until daybreak and then pushed off for the shore. Shortly before leaving the Captain removed his life-belt and gave it to the German Boy, saying 'Let there be one saved; here, my boy, take this.'

They were not far from the land when all three boats were hit by breakers. The boats were all swamped and only four were saved, the boy being one of them. The Captain, nine of the crew and Ellen Watkins were drowned and the only survivors were a Swedish and a Liverpudlian seaman, the boy and a woman passenger Bridget Burns of Clonmel, County Tipperary.

The WAPELLA did not break up straight away. In fact many people were of the opinion that had they all remained on board for a few more hours that they could have been rescued by the Lifeboat. The Lloyd's agent was informed and a crew experienced in unloading was sent from Liverpool to salvage the bales of cotton.
When the team arrived at Ardudwy they were not welcomed and they had difficulty in finding accommodation. The Caernarvon and Denbigh Herald reports; 'None of the inhabitants of the coast would give the poor fellows a night's lodgings, partly from the fear of them, and partly also from jealousy that the men from a distance had been sent for, instead of employing the natives. Great praise is due to Mrs Roberts, King's Head, Dyffryn, for her exertions to find lodgings, when all refused, she flung her house open for them to sleep on the floor.'

As it happened, a gale sprang up at the end of the week, before they had properly commenced the work, and only 700 bales of cotton were recovered. Had the local men been employed it was generally considered that the whole of the cotton cargo would have been saved.

The newspaper made a final comment, 'It is rumoured that there was much drunkenness amongst some of the inhabitants of the neighbourhood, who found some casks of rum on the shore.'

The American barque WAPELLA lost near Barmouth in 1868 would have looked similar to this sailing ship
Illustration: Illustrated London News

Wreck List
of those in this book and those included in Volume One

Ship Name	Date of Loss	Type	Location	Vol.	Page
ADAMANTIOS J PITHIS	1940	SS	ST. ANN'S HEAD	1	13
AILSA	1880	SS	ST. GOVAN'S HEAD	2	9
ALBION	1837	PS	WEST PEMBROKESHIRE	1	15
ALICE WILLIAMS	1928	SC	SKOKHOLM ISLAND	2	10
AMAZON	1908	BQ	MARGAM, GLAMORGAN	1	17
AMAZONENSE	1881	SS	NR. ST DAVID'S HEAD	1	19
ANN	1858	FLT	ST. TUDWAL'S ISLAND	2	12
AUSTRALIA	1901	BQ	CARMARTHEN BAY	2	13
BARON ARDROSSAN	1898	SS	NEAR ST DAVID'S HEAD	1	21
BRONWEN	1891	SC	NEW QUAY	2	15
CAESAR	1760	S	GOWER	1	23
CALBURGA	1915	BQ	NEAR STRUMBLE HEAD	2	17
CAMBRO	1913	SS	SMALLS	2	20
CHARLES HOLMES	1859	BQ	NORTH PEMBROKESHIRE	2	22
CITY OF BRISTOL	1840	PS	GOWER	1	25
COUNT D'ASPREMONT	1903	SS	RAMSEY SOUND	2	24
CRAIGWHINNIE	1899	BQ	CARMARTHEN BAY	1	27
CRESSWELL	1881	BQ	GOWER	2	27
DAKOTA	1877	SS	WEST ANGLESEY	1	29
DAKOTIAN	1940	SS	MILFORD HAVEN	1	31
DALSERF	1910	SS	GRASSHOLM	2	28
DAN BEARD	1944	SS	NEAR STRUMBLE HEAD	1	33
DUISBERG	1899	BQ	GOWER	1	35
ELLERBECK	1914	SS	OFF PEMBROKESHIRE	1	37
ELTAMBO	1977	SS	FISHGUARD	2	32
FARADAY	1941	SS	WEST PEMBROKESHIRE	1	39
FELLSIDE	1924	SS	GOWER	2	33
FLYING FOAM	1936	SC	LLANDUDNO	1	41
FORT MEDINE	1941	SS	SWANSEA BAY	2	35
FROLIC	1831	PS	NASH SANDS	1	42
GILBERT THOMPSON	1881	BQ	CEMLYN, ANGLESEY	2	36
GLENISLA	1886	SS	ABEREIDDY, PEMBROKESHIRE	2	38
GOVERNOR FENNER	1841	FRS	OFF HOLYHEAD	2	41
GRAFFOE	1903	SS	RAMSEY ISLAND	1	44
GRAMSBERGEN	1954	MV	FISHGUARD	1	46
HAROLD	1908	SS	WEST ANGLESEY	1	49

Ship Name	Date of Loss	Type	Location	Vol.	Page
HELVETIA	1887	BQ	RHOSSILI, GOWER	2	42
HEREFORDSHIRE	1934	SS	CARDIGAN ISLAND	1	51
HERMINA	1920	SC	FISHGUARD BAY	1	53
HINDLEA	1959	MV	MOELFRE, ANGLESEY	2	46
HMS BARKING	1964	BD	ST. ANN'S HEAD	2	44
HORNBY	1824	BG	LLANDUDNO	2	48
HUDIKSVALL	1890	BQ	CARMEL HEAD, ANGLESEY	2	49
JAMES GRAY	1883	SS	TUSKER, PORTHCAWL	1	55
KIRKMICHAEL	1894	BQ	HOLYHEAD	1	57
KITTY	1819	FRS	FISHGUARD	1	59
KYLE FIRTH	1940	SS	NEAR HOLYHEAD	1	60
KYLE PRINCE	1940	SS	ABERFFRAW, ANGLESEY	2	51
LA JEUNE EMMA	1828	BG	CARMARTHEN BAY	1	61
LANCASTER	1835	FRS	CARDIGAN BAY	1	63
LANGTON GRANGE	1909	SS	NEAR ST DAVID'S	1	64
LA PLATA	1863	BQ	OFF POINT LYNAS	1	68
LEYSIAN	1917	SS	ABERCASTLE, PEMBROKESHIRE	2	53
LINNET	1890	SM	BEAUMARIS, ANGLESEY	2	55
LIVERPOOL	1863	SS	OFF POINT LYNAS	1	68
LUCY	1967	MV	SKOMER ISLAND	1	73
LUMINENCE	1967	MV	HATS & BARRELS	2	56
MARY	1675	RY	SKERRIES	2	58
MERKUR	1920	SS	OFF BARRY	1	76
MISSOURI	1886	SS	NEAR HOLYHEAD	2	59
MOLESEY	1929	SS	NEAR SKOMER ISLAND	1	77
MYSTIC TIE	1877	BGN	RAMSEY ISLAND	2	62
NETHERHOLME	1907	SS	LINNEY HEAD	2	64
NIMROD	1860	PS	ST. DAVID'S HEAD	2	65
NORMAN COURT	1883	BQ	NEAR HOLYHEAD	1	79
NUEVO TORCUVATA	1856	BQ	SAUNDERSFOOT	2	68
OCEAN	1895	SM	CARDIGAN	2	70
OLINE	1882	SC	NEWPORT PEMBROKESIRE	1	81
OLINDA	1854	SS	CEMLYN, ANGLESEY	2	71
OWEN MORRIS	1907	SC	PORTHMADOG	1	83
PAUL	1925	SC	CARMARTHEN BAY	1	84
PILOT CUTTER No.5	1881	CUT	OFF LAVERNOCK POINT	1	85
PRINCE CADWGAN	1876	SS	NEAR RAMSEY SOUND	2	73
PRINCESS IRENE	1906	SS	LINNEY HEAD	2	74
RAGNA	1900	BQ	TREFIN, PEMBROKESHIRE	2	76
RENE	1886	BQ	GOWER	1	87

Ship Name	Date of Loss	Type	Location	Vol.	Page
RESURGAM	1880	SUB	OFF RHYL	2	79
RHOSNEIGR	1908	PS	RHOS ON SEA	2	81
ROCHE CASTLE	1937	MV	GOWER	2	82
ROTHSAY CASTLE	1831	PS	OFF BEAUMARIS	1	88
ROYAL CHARTER	1859	SS	ANGLESEY	1	90
SALUS	1896	BQN	STRUMBLE HEAD	1	93
SAMTAMPA	1947	SS	PORTHCAWL	1	95
SHEPTON MALLET	1731	S	GOWER	1	97
STEEPHOLM	1968	MV	TUSKER ROCK	2	84
STRATHALLAN	1887	SS	LAVERNOCK POINT	2	86
STUART	1901	BQ	LLEYN	1	98
SZENT ISTVAN	1908	SS	RAMSEY ISLAND	2	87
THETIS	1939	SUB	OFF POINT LYNAS	1	100
TIMBO	1920	SS	CAERNARFON BAY	2	90
TIVYSIDE	1900	SS	GOWER	2	92
TRELAWNY	1806	FRS	NASH POINT	1	102
TRIDONIA	1916	BQ	GOWER	2	94
TWELVE APOSTLES	1898	SC	PWLLHELI	2	96
VAINQUEUR	1753	S	PORTHCAWL	1	103
VALSESIA	1926	SS	BARRY	2	98
VERNICOS TUGS	1981	TUG	SOLVA, PEMBROKESHIRE	2	99
WAPELLA	1868	BQ	BARMOUTH	2	102
ZELO	1920	SS	OFF BARRY	1	76

Abbreviations used for ship type

BD . . . . BOOM DEFENCE
BG . . . . BRIG
BGN . . . . . . BRIGANTINE
BQ . . . . BARQUE
BQN . . . . . . BARQUENTINE
CUT . . . . CUTTER RIG
FLT . . . . SAILING FLAT
FRS . . . . FULL RIGGED SHIP
MFV . . . . . . MOTOR FISHING VESSEL
MV . . . . MOTOR VESSEL
PS . . . . PADDLE STEAMER
RY . . . . ROYAL YACHT
S . . . . SAILING VESSEL
SC . . . . SCHOONER
SS . . . . STEAMSHIP
SUB . . . . SUBMARINE
TUG . . . . TUG

Bibliography

BENNETT, T.H. Fishguard Lifeboats, (Fishguard & Goodwick Ladies' Lifeboat Guild, 1984)
British Vessels Lost at Sea, 1939-1945 (Patrick Stephens, 1976)
BSAC Wreck Register, Wales, Isle of Man & Ireland (British Sub Aqua Club, 1984)
EDMUNDS, G. The Gower Coast, (Regional Publications, 1979)
EAMES, A. & HUGHES,E. Porthmadog Ships, (Gwynedd Archives Service, 1975)
EAMES, A. Ships and Seamen of Anglesey, (Anglesey Antiquarian Society, 1979)
ELIS-WILLIAMS, M. Bangor, Port of Beaumaris, (Gwynedd Archives, 1988)
EVANS, A.L, Some Pirates, Smugglers & Wrecks in the Bristol Channel, (Port Talbot, 1984)
FARR, G. Wreck & Rescue in the Bristol Channel 11, (Bradford Barton,Truro, 1967)
FARR, G. Shipbuilding in the Port of Bristol, (National Maritime Museum, No.27, 1977)
FENTON, R. A Historical Tour Through Pembrokeshire, (1811)
FENTON, R.S. Cambrian Coasters, (World Ship Society,1989)
GODDARD, T. Pembrokeshire Shipwrecks, (Hughes, 1983)
HOCKING, C.A. A Dictionary of Disasters at Sea in the Age of Steam, 1824-1962, 1 & 11, (Lloyds, 1969)
HOOKE, N. Modern Shipping Disasters, 1963-1987, (Lloyds of London Press Ltd, 1989)
HOWELLS, R. Across the Sounds to the Pembrokeshire Islands, (Gomer, 1982)
HOWELLS, R. The Sounds Between, (H.G.Walters, 1968)
JENKINS, J.G. Maritime Heritage, (Gomer, 1982)
JONES, I.W, Shipwrecks of North Wales, (David & Charles, 1973)
LARN, R. Shipwrecks of Great Britain and Ireland, (David & Charles, 1981)
LEWIS, E.A. The Welsh Port Books 1550-1603, (1927)
LUBBOCK, B. The Colonial Clippers, (J.Brown & Son,Glasgow, 1921)
Maritime Wales, Cymru A'r Môr, Nos. 1 to 14 (Gwynedd Archives Service, 1977 to 1991)
McALISTER. A.A. H.Hogarth & Sons, (World Ship Society, 1976)
MORRIS, J. Tenby Lifeboats, (Tenby Station Branch, 1989)
MORRIS, J. The Story of the Holyhead Lifeboats, (Coventry, 1979)
MORRIS, W. Plans of Harbours, etc., St George's & Bristol Channels, (Shrewsbury, 1801).
NICHOLSON, J.A. Pembrey & Burry Port, Their Harbours, Shipwrecks and Looters, (Llanelli Borough Council, 1985)
Old Port Talbot & District in Photographs Vol 1, (Port Talbot Historical Society, 1979)
PARRY, H. Wreck & Rescue on the Coast of Wales,1, (Bradford Barton,Truro, 1969)
REES, P.H. Gower Shipwrecks, (C.Davies, 1978)
ROSCOE, T. Wanderings & Excursions in South Wales, (London, 1844)
SKIDMORE, I. Anglesey & Lleyn Shipwrecks, (C.Davies, 1979)
SMITH, C. The Men of Mumbles Head, (Gower Press, 1977)
West Coasts of England & Wales Pilot (Hydrographer of the Navy, 1974)
ZANELLI, L. Shipwrecks Around Britain, (Kaye & Ward, 1970)
ZANELLI, L. Unknown Shipwrecks Around Britain, (Kaye & Ward, 1974)

Newspapers, Magazines & Other References.

Board of Trade Annual Returns of Shipping Casualties
Brown's Nautical Almanac 1889
Caernarfon & Denbigh Herald, various dates
Cambrian News, from 1808
Cardiff Times, 1858 to 1928
Cardigan & Tivyside Advertiser, various dates from 1897
Carmarthen Journal, from 1912
County Echo, from 1893

Dewisland & Kemes Guardian, 1861 to 1882
Diver magazine, from 1980
Flintshire Herald
Graphic, 1869 to 1901
Haverfordwest & Milford Haven Telegraph, 1854 to 1919
Illustrated London News, 1842 to 1900
Lloyds Manuscript Wreck Registers, 1855 to 1895
Lloyds Register of Ships, from 1764
Lloyds List, 1741 to 1826

Nautical Magazine
Pembrokeshire Herald, 1844 to 1924
Red Dragon, 1882 to 1887
Sea Breezes, from 1932
South Wales Press, 1867 to 1934
The Times, from 1788
The Lifeboat, RNLI quarterly
Welshman, from 1829
Western Daily Press, from 1858
Western Mail & Echo, from 1869
Western Telegraph, from 1937
West Wales Guardian, from 1927

Index

Ships and Lifeboats are in capitals.
For surnames of Captains look under the heading of Captain.

Location Map of Wrecks in Volume 1

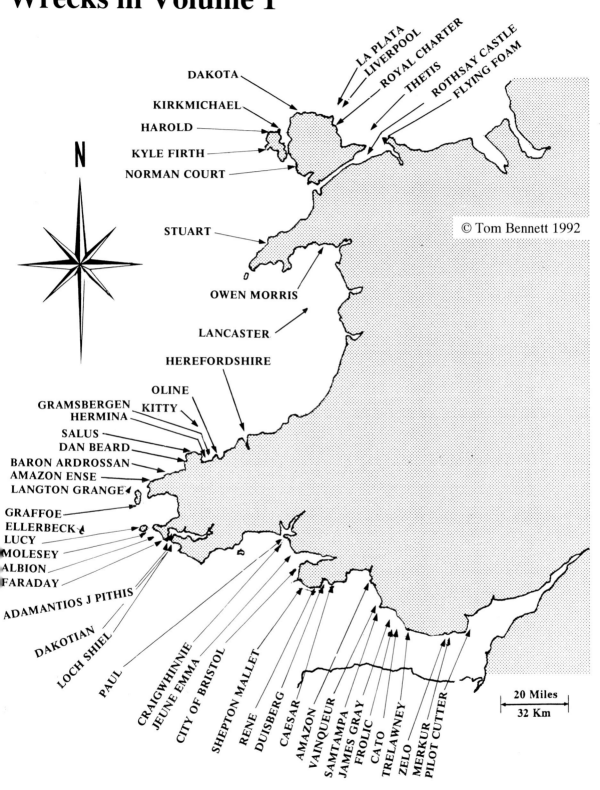

DAKOTA
KIRKMICHAEL
HAROLD
KYLE FIRTH
NORMAN COURT

LA PLATA
LIVERPOOL
ROYAL CHARTER
THETIS
ROTHSAY CASTLE
FLYING FOAM

N

© Tom Bennett 1992

STUART

OWEN MORRIS

LANCASTER

HEREFORDSHIRE

OLINE
GRAMSBERGEN   KITTY
HERMINA
SALUS
DAN BEARD
BARON ARDROSSAN
AMAZON ENSE
LANGTON GRANGE

GRAFFOE
ELLERBECK
LUCY
MOLESEY
ALBION
FARADAY

ADAMANTIOS J PITHIS

DAKOTIAN

LOCH SHIEL

PAUL

CRAIGWHINNIE
JEUNE EMMA
CITY OF BRISTOL

SHEPTON MALLET

RENE
DUISBERG
CAESAR

AMAZON
VAINQUEUR
SAMTAMPA
JAMES GRAY
FROLIC
CATO
TRELAWNEY
ZELO
MERKUR
PILOT CUTTER

20 Miles
32 Km

111

About the Author

Tom Bennett resides in Newport, Pembrokeshire, a short walk away from the waters of Cardigan Bay. He is an Environmental Health Officer with Preseli Pembrokeshire District Council. For over twenty years he has been enthusiastically collecting details of shipwrecks around Wales and has dived on many of the wreck sites that he writes about. He holds a full Yachtmaster (Offshore) Certificate, is a past Commodore of Fishguard Bay Yacht Club and has sailed in and out of most of the harbours of Wales, the east coast of Ireland and the Bristol Channel.

What was said of Volume One.

'Generously illustrated with photographs and pictures of the wrecks and artefacts recovered, this book also includes many wreck location maps. These, together with the ship details, provide a useful record and a unique reference book for all who are interested in shipwrecks around Wales.'

The Book Journal, Autumn 1989.

'A thorough index makes the book a useful and valuable reference apart from its general interest.'

Alan Cameron, Lloyds List, September 5th 1987.

'. . . accurately researched, well illustrated book in which the author's enthusiasm for his subject comes through to the reader.'

Sea Breezes, September 1987.

'The numerous photographs, drawings, maps and diagrams make this a most comprehensive guide so that one eagerly awaits Volume 2.'

David Saunders, The West Wales Guardian, June 5th 1987.

Tom Bennett studies a model of the CALBURGA at the Maritime Museum of the Atlantic. The CALBURGA was the last square rigged ship to be registered in Halifax, Nova Scotia. She was lost near Strumble Head in 1915 and sank in 40 metres of water, the author discovered the wreck site in 1975.
Photo: Maritime Museum of the Atlantic, Halifax, Nova Scotia.